Wednesfield Our Heritage

Ray Fellows

Published 2011

ISBN 978-178035-221-3

Printed by
Printondemand-Worldwide.com

To contact Ray with your memories

Telephone: (01902) 739592)

Email: fellows.raymond@yahoo.co.uk

Contents

Illustrations

Introduction

Once again 'It's yesterday once more'. Welcome to my third book about the history of Wednesfield. I hope that you can relate to some of the stories and illustrations that appear in this book.
Again, we have other people's memories of their time spent in Wednesfield under the section of Speakers Corner. It has been great to get people talking about Wednesfield Our Village and the views that appeared in my two previous books. It should be helpful to those who wish to know and understand Wednesfield better and convince them that the battle between the Saxons and Danes took place here in Wednesfield Our Wednesfield.
Special thanks to Mrs Elizabeth Smallshire for granting permission to use some of her late husband John's photographs; also to Mr and Mrs Stride.
My thanks and appreciation go to my wife Kath for being so understanding and supportive and to those folk that have contriubuted to Speakers Corner. Also thanks go to the staff at Wolverhampton Archives and Wednesfield Library and finally to my daughter Stephanie for putting this book together. I thank you all.
Ray Fellows
2011

1. Wednesfield 1879

Wednesfield is a township and chapelry in the south division of Offlow Hundred, 2 miles NE of Wolverhampton and on the Wyrley and Essington Canal; it contains upwards of 3000 acres of land.
Immense quantities of locks, keys and traps of every description are manufactured here for the Birmingham and Wolverhampton merchants. In the Domesday Book this place is called Wodensfelde (from Woden the Saxon God of Battle) and is mentioned among the lands given to Wulfruna's monastery.
It is memorable as the scene of a decisive victory which Edward the Elder obtained over the Danes in 910AD; and which is thus related by Dr Plott after his account of the Battle of Tettenhall where the Danes were also routed with dreadful slaughter: "Another Army of the Danes that possessed Northumberland, breaking a league they had formerly made with King Edward, invaded Mercia in the very same year, pillaging the country wherever they came; against whom, King Edward, bringing a powerful Army both of West Saxons and Mercians overtook them in their return at the village of Wednesfield, not far from Tettenhall and overthrew them again in another bloody battle, wherein he killed Eowills and Halfden, Hildein, two of their Kings and Ohter and Scurfa, two of their Earls and nine other noblemen to whom Ethelwardus adds Fuver or Hinguar another of their Kings: of which great slaughter there are no more remains but a low called Southlow-field and another called Northlow-field. These doubtless were cast up over some of those Kings, or Danish or Saxon Nobles, then Slain here."

2. Wednesfield 1896

In 1896 Wednesfield had 20 Trap makers, 55 Keymakers, 26 Beer retailers, 24 Farmers, 19 Lockmakers, 5 Coal merchants, also Ashmore Park Colliery Co Limited with James Broughall as manager. There were two pawnbrokers; Thomas Griffiths of Rookery Street and Thomas Hickman of Taylor Street.
Staffordshire Constabulary New Cross (sub-division) one Sergeant and 7 Constables, Sergeant in charge Frank Biddulph.

Railway Station Midland, John Grundy, Station Master. Heath Town, Herbert Peat, Station Master.

Wednesfield had 2 Blacksmiths, Arkinstall of Long Knowle Lane and Joseph Turner Blacksmiths wheelwright of Church Street. We had David Austin who was a Fishmonger in Church Street and Thomas Nicholls fish and chip shop in Rookery Street. We had a couple of Tailors; James Snape, High Street and Lester Hollins of Church Street. A couple of Bakers, Sarah Evans (Mrs) of Hickman Street and of course James William Done High Street. Thomas Beech, Shopkeeper Wood End. Can you recall their shop? The Beech's must have had that shop for quite some time because I can remember the shop when I was a kid. If you think about it we still have similar shops today in roughly the same places; a fish shop in Church Street and one on Rookery Street. Pubs are in the same places except for those that are no more; Royal Oak, Rose and Crown and the Lion. All now gone but I am sure that you will agree that there are plenty of pubs left. What is the name of Wednesfield's newest pub?

Well we all should know the oldest pub in Wednesfield; it's the Dog and Partridge.

3. Wednesfield 1948 – 1950

A stranger approaching Wednesfield for the first time will probably do so via the main Wolverhampton – Bloxwich Road. The distance is only two miles – a three penny ride on the trolley bus and the feeling of turning ones back on Wolverhampton was not immediately apparent. Just beyond New Cross Hospital however, a hump backed bridge over the canal affords a momentary glimpse of the general lie of the town, and very soon the narrow high street and the cluster of houses built around the parish church unmistakeably reveal Wednesfield's village origin.

A brief stay in the town will also reveal equally unmistakeably, that Wednesfield was in every sense a separate community, exhibiting sturdy independence and a strong sense of civic pride. These virtues, desirably in any town have been stimulated in Wednesfield by threats of encroachment and absorption by neighbouring towns.

Wednesfield is one of the oldest, if not the oldest of the Black Country townships, for it has had a separate existence and identity for upwards of a thousand years. In 910 a fierce battle was fought here between the Saxons, led by Edward the Elder and the Danes; the result being an overwhelming defeat for the latter. The Saxons named the battle area Wodensfield in honour of their war God 'Woden' hence the present name.

Wednesfields historical background has been perpetuated in the design of the civic seal of the Urban Distract Council and the design can be seen to advantage in the Chairman's Badge of office in which the artist has portrayed the warriors at the height of the battle.

Doomsday book; the great national land register in which was entered the ownership, condition and annual value of every acre of land in England, sets down among the possessions of the cannons of Wolverhampton that of 2,200 acres in Wednesfield. It is interesting to note that the area at that time (1086) is remarkably close to the present area of 2,515 acres.

Wednesfield U D C Coat of Arms

Fig.1. Wednesfield UDC coat of arms

The battle of 910 appears to be Wednesfields only contribution to history and up to the eighteenth century it remained a small hamlet whose inhabitants zealously guarded their independence against encroachment by those neighbouring hamlets.

Even at the annual 'Wakes' events when cock fighting was not least amongst the attractions, spontaneous pugilistic bouts were indulged in by all and sundry. With the opening of the canals about 1750 however, and the railway in the following century, the tide of industry which had already covered some of the fairest parts of Staffordshire reached Wednesfield.

That was written in Wednesfields official guide 1948 – 1950, I particularly like the part about the battle taking place here in 910. I have to say this; I have been telling everyone that I meet that the evidence of where the famous battle took place is overwhelmingly in favour of here our Wednesfield, now believe it; it is true that the battle took place here in 910.

The Jorvic Viking Festival held in York in February 2010 reconstructed a bloody battle recreating the aftermath of the battle of Wodens Field and that it happened in 910AD when three Viking Kings left their stronghold in York to carry out raids in the Midlands and South West. As they returned from the raid the King of Wessex caught up with them near Wolverhampton, taking them by surprise and killing thousands, including all three Viking Kings.

Verna Johansen of Cookley near Kidderminster said the Anglo Saxon Chronicles New Edition backs up claims that events tool place in Wednesfield, reporting: 'They (the Vikings) harried through Mercia and over the Severn into the West Country.'

4. The Battle

'But when rejoicing in rich spoil, they were in the process of crossing back over the Severn Bridge; they were attacked by squadrons of both Mercians and West Saxons, which on the 5th August gained a great victory on Wodens Field (Wednesfield) killing three Viking Kings.'

For me the evidence is overwhelming. There is one other thing that you might like to think about and that is this; The Vikings left their stronghold in York to carry out raids in the Midlands and South West. Well they did not come down here and the South West for the fresh air, they came to loot and get anything that was of any value and on this they must have had a huge haul of gold that they had plundered from around the Midlands and the South West. So what happened to all of that gold? Could it be that all the gold and valuable possessions that the Vikings had ended up in the hands of the Saxons? Well that part is obvious as the Saxons won the battle and any valuables would not have been left in Wednesfield. So where would they have been taken? Let's look at it this way. We had Mercians here in the Midlands and Wessex down south, where's the nearest Mercian stronghold? Tamworth is a lot closer than Wessex so the booty would go to Tamworth; Elfleda's home. But what happened on the way to Tamworth? As no-one knows how much gold and valuable possessions the Saxons ended up with, could it have been a case of greed by some of the Saxons on the way back to Tamworth? Did some of the soldiers and the higher ranking officials decide to hide part of the haul in a field near Brownhills believing that they could come back to it later? Just take some of the gold to Tamworth Castle. Who's to know how much of it there was? That could well have been the case, after all most of you have heard of the Staffordshire hoard, where a chap found all that gold with his metal detecter. The time period is roughly the same time, although it's hard to put a precise date on the gold, it is around the same time as the battle.

The find by the metal detecter enthusiast is now in the Birmingham Museum. We would like to take a look at the find, we know the site of the find, and it is just off the A5 on the road to Tamworth.

This is speculation but could it be that those soldiers and officials who were not involved in hiding the hoard returned to Tamworth to find the gold and all the other valuables that were taken at Wednesfield were not all there and that those trusted with taking the gold and valuables to Tamworth were executed and never gave up where they had buried the gold. It's certainly worth considering because we know that the Vikings had been on raids and they would have had a haul of valuables and so what could have happened to the hoard? It seems to fit just like a jigsaw puzzle.

Well that's my theory anyway, what do you think? It has been my passion to prove that the famous battle took place in 910AD in Our Wednesfield. You say you want to seek the truth but it is hard to find. No-one to help you, your friends don't have the time but it's been put in front of you now make your own minds up. I didn't think of all this

when I was a kid, but when you get older you tend to look at things differently. The place where I live was a place where a famous battle took place on the 5/6th August 910AD.
Since writing this piece I have since talked to Archaeologists at Tamworth and they tell me that the Staffordshire hoard is from the 5th to the 7th Century and that it is early Saxon.
Yes I can accept that part after all they are a lot wiser than me about that sort of thing but hey, the hoard is around today so obviously it was around in the 10th Century, the experts in saying that the gold hoard dates from 5 / 7thy Century, yes but it does not mean that it was buried then, the hoard could be from all around England and could have been plundered by the Vikings and buried at any time by either the Vikings or the Saxons.
It seems that the Staffordshire hoard dates to the reign of the greatest Saxon King of all, PENDA who reined in the early 600s.

Fig.2.Site of Battle between Saxons and Vikings August 5th / 6th 910AD

Fig.3. Imposing: Tamworth Castle; home of Elfleda, Lady of Mercian's.

5. Wednesfield Church

Fig.4. The Church after the fire of 1902.

This picture shows the devastation that the fire caused to St Thomas' on Saturday evening January 18th 1902. The Church was rebuilt using the outer walls and tower and it was reopened in 1903.

Fig.5. Church after the fire of 1902.

Fig.6. Church, view from Graiseley Lane early 1900's.

Fig.7. Church Bridge. Chimney of the Boat on the left. A gathering for the photo, those old cottages were demolished and the library was built in 1955.

Fig.8. Wednesfield Church 1950's.

Fig.9. View of Church from Graiseley Lane.

6. Christmas

Christmas is the most wonderful time of the year especially for the kids. You try to save a bit each week as the big day gets nearer you make your lists of who to send Christmas cards to and who you are going to buy presents for, not forgetting that it cost a small fortune last year. I can hear you saying next year we will have to cut back a bit.

We all have the same ideas about sending cards and buying presents, the only thing different is that another year rolls by. They seem to be coming quicker as you get older but nonetheless we still look forward to it. January has just gone by, we are now at February 5th, and it has gone so quick since Christmas. It is right what they say; time waits for no man. Before we know it we will be sweltering in those hot temperatures we get in July and August. A few months after that we will be thinking of getting the tree back down from the attic. Was it worth putting it back up? It has only been there since the 12th night of Christmas. What does Christmas mean to you? Could it be that you will be entertaining relatives and friends over the festive period or would you sooner be going around theirs for a few drinks and celebrations. People tend to differ at Christmas time, some like to go on holiday, but really speaking Christmas is a time to be spent with the family and friends. We have never really had the opportunity to go away at Christmas, but we prefer to stay at home. Midnight mass for Kath and Steph, it's the TV and a pint for me and reflecting on what has happened over the last 12 months. Not a lot really, work takes up most of my time, the same as most people I suppose. It's just the same for working folk, go to work, come home and do a bit of shopping, cook the tea, watch the soaps and off to bed. This is to be repeated the next day until you get to Friday. The weekend gives us a break from the daily routine that we all take part in. Anyway back to Christmas, as your kids have grown up we now embrace the grandkids. It's just like when our kids were small, it's great. Buying them presents and seeing their faces when they sit and open them. You will find that most families do the same at Christmas. Get up early and put the turkey in the oven, get all the veg prepared then the presents can be opened. We are lucky at the moment because our daughter Steph and son Chris are still living at home. Our other son Ben is married and living down by New Invention. Aint it marvellous we don't want them to leave. I suppose it's the same for most families you just don't want them to leave the nest because once they do everything will seem different. No more arguments about who will do the washing up or hoovering, put this away or who made this mess? Yes I know what you are thinking but we really love it don't we. Christmas morning is over so it's down to the Dog and Partridge for a couple of pints while the turkey cooks away in the oven. A couple of pints with our neighbours and friends usually turns into three or four drinks, then it's a bit of a panic to get home to get the dinner sorted. It is usually about 2:30 – 3:00 that we sit down to eat. You buy a big turkey and a piece of beef and after the meal there's loads left...turkey sandwiches, turkey stew, and turkey curry. You name it you can do it. Buy a smaller turkey next year because you are just wasting money. You know you will still buy a big one to make sure there is enough to go around. Do you think the same as us? The TV is useless, nothing any good on. What has happened to the Christmas's we used to have? Good old black and white films, Dickens Christmas Carol but not the modern versions they are rubbish. I don't think the Snowman was on this year, I might have missed it. No matter, we have it on DVD anyway. Probably watch it in the summer so that we are getting prepared for Christmas.

I will say this about Christmas; it's a very emotional time when you think of loved ones who are no longer with us. Everyone in some way is affected by the feelings that we get at that time of year. It brings a tear to your eyes when you reflect on the friends and even members of the family that we have lost not only over the last twelve months but it might be ten, twenty, thirty or more years since you last saw them but you can still picture them. One thing's for sure, they will never be forgotten. There will always be a place in our hearts for them no matter how long they have been gone. Our memories might fade but we will never forget them. God rest the folk that have been here and are now departed from this world. Please Lord; help them to rest in peace.

I told you that Christmas is a very emotional time; well you had better believe it.

Merry Christmas and a Happy New Year and always remember it is better to give than receive and whoever said that must have more money than sense.

Christmas is really for the kids. When you were a kid did you believe in Father Christmas? Yes you did. When did you stop believing? Or do you still believe in him? I think that I was about ten or eleven but you are not sure as a kid. Anyway for any kids that might be reading this, Father Christmas does exist it's just that when you grow older you think more important things than Father Christmas. It's just a mental thing with us grown-ups. When we really get old then we really want to go back to believing that Father Christmas exists, it's just that we want different types of presents than those we had when we were kids and perhaps we want to go back to those happy days when you were a kid and loved and respected your parents. That is what memories are made of...families and friends from the past. If you live to receive the Queens telegram you will never forget the good times that you had in your early years. How far back can you remember? I can just about recall being aged five and being in the Neachells Lane Infant School. Can you recall your earliest time at school? If you can then who were your teachers? Name one if you can, yes you can do it. Think about the past, in particular those wonderful days spent at school. I can remember making trimmings at Lichfield Road School, you know those pieces where you would lick one end and stick them together and you could make a train to hang up. Do they still do them now?

Did you ever do any carol singing when you were a kid? I mean around the streets or even in pubs. Well I did and I thoroughly enjoyed it. Hey and the money was great, people used to be fairly generous when I was a kid. I could sing then, it used to be: Silent Night or Once in Royal David's City. Easy songs to remember, can you remember the words now? No, I can't either but never mind, you can always go to a carol concert at the Grandkids school, you will soon pick it up or perhaps pop into Wednesfield Village and listen to the music from the Rotary Club's sleigh. It is great of them to put this on for our benefit. What about Ruth Badger switching on the lights for Wednesfield, absoloutly brilliant. I did my book signing in the library on Friday 17th December 2010. It was great to be able to use the library to sign books about Wednesfield. Where else could I have done it? And what about the Christmas tree by the library, brilliant. We must thank Simon Hamilton and members of his staff for that. Same again this year please.

I did a couple of hours on the market with my book; 'This is Wednesfield Our Wednesfield'. I will tell you this, I was absolutely frozen. I ended up in the Dog and Partridge having a whisky to chill myself out, purely medicinal of course! I don't think I could go back to working on the markets especially in that weather. Let's not forget that it is one of the coldest winters we have had in a long time. I've just had a thought; our gas bill is going to be something like £500. I kept telling Kath to turn the heating down but she would not listen. "It's cold" she said. "Yes I know it is but we have to keep the bill down". No chance really if it's cold then put the central heating on and the gas fire. Blimey if you are reading this it must mean that we somehow paid the gas bill. At the time of writing I can't see how we

are going to do it. We are like most families, it's a struggle to pay the bills and keep on top of things. I would like to ask readers a question. If I get a pay rise of 3%, my gas bills goes up by 18% and electric by 11%, then we have VAT going up to 20%, then how can we as hard working folk make ends meet? Is it really worth going to work? It seems to me that the poor get poorer and the rich get richer. Value Added Tax is the biggest rip off since the Poll Tax was introduced by Maggie. That resulted in riots. What is Value Added Tax? We want to heat our house so that's value that we are getting; at the prices I doubt it. We want to use electric to switch a light on so we have to pay VAT. It's not value it's just a big rip off. We need to rewind to Oliver Cromwell's days and ask him about VAT. What about it Oliver? Do you have any comments?
When you look at it, this country is being torn apart by greed. Banks are the biggest culprits, better be careful what I say, they might call in my overdraft, but really it does not matter which party is in power they are all the same; promises and good intentions turn out to be nothing more than here say. "No we were misquoted" they say; sorry I am getting carried away with how I feel about our economy. And on that, a final note is we must pay the highest price for petrol anywhere. What's happened to the North Sea oil that we had? When will we see the benefits? After all it's on our doorstep and not in the Middle East. I can bet you this; if anyone invented something that made your car run on fresh air then the government would want to tax it. Unfortunately that's the type of thing that we tax payers have to put up with. Sorry for the moaning but someone has to say something. It just seems that whatever government is in power they just want to put the squeeze on the poor folk of the country. On that note here endeth the lesson.
The Pied Piper by Crispian St Peters says it all in 1966. Follow me and I'll show you where it's at. Can't you see I'm the Pied Piper? The record 'He aint heavy....He's my brother' by the Hollies will always be remembered by my family. As a lot of people know, I lost my brother in 1968. Ron was a better person than I will ever be but the Lord decided that he wanted to take him rather than me. Even he knows that he did not deserve to go at the age of 15. Why? Why? Why?

Try playing a record from the 60's and then you can relate to the events and activities of the real times. Try playing 'Eve of Destruction' by Barry McGuire 1965, if the button is pushed then there's no running away. This whole crazy world is just too frustrating and you can tell me over and over and over again my friend that you don't believe we're on the eve of destruction.

7. Stories of old Wednesfield

One of the best known Wednesfield characters of some sixty / eighty years ago was 'Dennis'. He was a man so thin that repute has it that if he was standing near to a lamppost, anyone on the other side could not see him, yet he had an enormous appetite. A story is told in the locals of an occasion when he was 'instructed' as the results of a wager, to sit down to a meal of forty faggots and a jug of gravy. He had to admit defeat however, after eating less than half. It was said that his size had increased so much that had he eaten more, the door of the pub would have had to be removed to enable him to leave. Do you remember the film 'Cool Hand Luke' with Paul Newman eating fifty boiled eggs? Well this had got to be on a par with that.
Back to the story about Dennis, on another occasion he was challenged to eat a certain quantity of cheese without bread. He arrived at the battleground half an hour too soon, whereupon someone fetched half a pound of cheese 'for practise'. This was duly consumed and then in the actual contest he consumed a further one and a half pounds. Dennis was thought by some to be something of a walker and he was once backed against another man to walk from Wednesfield Church to Four Ashes and back. As he was stepping out near to 'The Harrows' on Stafford Road he suddenly came across his opponent on the return journey. So Dennis gave up and completed his return to Wednesfield on the cross bar of a kindly cyclist.
The last occasion on which he was known to compete in a walking match was during one of the annual 'stay at home' holiday programmes during the last war. A race had been organised at the 'Pear Tree' to the King George V playing fields finishing by a complete circuit of the field. Let's not forget that back then in 1953 Dennis was 57 years of age and was well behind the other eight competitors

when he arrived at the gates but everyone was cheering him on: "Come on Dennis!", "Good old Dennis" cried the crowd. About twenty yards from the gate he stumbled and fell. Frightened supporters ran to him and found him in a rather bad way. Someone fetched the organiser of the race, who on arrival called out "Are you alright Dennis? Speak to me Dennis! If only you would get up I'll see that you sing on the platform and have a collection for you!" At these heartening words Dennis made a sudden and wonderful recovery and ten minutes later was singing lustily in front of the microphone. When the promised collection was taken for him his popularity was proved for he received more money than the entire prize winners put together. Dennis was liked everywhere. He never fell out with anyone, he never argued and his memory will live for many years.

Stories of old 'Wedgefelt.'

Many years ago Wednesfield was reputed for its interest in sport; principally cock fighting, pigeon flying, whippet racing, dog fighting and rat catching. It was the ambition of most of the men to own a dog better than anyone else and by far what fine specimens were bred and trained. I used to take a dozen live rats to a venue at the corner of Wood End Road and Lichfield Road and bets were laid by dog owners as to which dog killed the first rat. I remember well when old Jack Petford bet that his dog would kill a rat in the kitchen of 'The Boat Inn'. There was no door to the cellar but just an opening. Jack Wallbanks, otherwise known as 'Longboat' held a big piece of cardboard to the opening to prevent the rat escaping. When, however I loosed the rat it immediately ran for the cardboard. Off went Longboat down the cellar chased by the rat. I followed but the rat ran up the pipes into the bar where there was further trouble, not the least of which was several broken glasses. Poor old Longboat was scared out of his wits.

A certain farmer in Wednesfield wanted someone to go along to his farm with a dog to dispose of some of his rats. George Bowyer told me that the farmer would pay four – pence per rat. Off Charlie (my friend) and I went and at the end of the day the farmer came to us and was able to count ninety seven dead vermin, apart from which we had nearly two cages of live ones. The farmer scared of the amount which he would have to pay disappeared into the house. I said to Charlie "He isn't going to pay us." We knocked at the door for quite a time and eventually the farmer came, whereupon Charlie put his big foot behind the door and forced it open. We emptied the live rats in what turned out to be the dairy, all nice and clean with white muslin over the churns. The farmer got panicky and offered us 10 shillings and some beer as thick as mud to catch them again. By the time all was finished that dairy looked more like a pigsty than anything else. (Signed) 'Bingy' W H Bodley.

It was a common sight in days gone by to see cages containing pet birds hanging outside people's houses. How proud the locals were to show off their hobby. I remember well a bird singing contest at the 'Rose and Crown'. It aroused so much interest that the police had to come and disperse the crowd. Beautiful cages were bought along that day – some of them fine enough to carry the crown jewels in. Some men paid as much as 20 shillings per lb. for bird seed and that at a time when beer was only 5d per pint. A friend of mine, who had a bird which he called 'Peace Day' was once offered and refused a twenty score pig in exchange for it. He admitted that he had won more than the value of the pig in contests.

A certain gentleman living in a fairly large house in Wednesfield was worried about noises which he was hearing underneath his house. Apparently the rabbits which infested his land had burrowed underneath. He invited my friends and me to do something about it so we went along with ferrets, my dog and a gun. The friend with the gun was instructed to shoot at the rabbits after they were ferreted out and shoot he did; just as a beautiful grey boat horse was hauling a boatload of coal around the turn of the canal near the house. Bang! Bang! Went the gun, the horse panicked, broke the line and jumped into the canal.

That was the very first time that I heard the 'Boatman's Prayer'. It took several hours to get that horse out of the canal. In the excitement we discovered that one of our ferrets was missing, but luckily, before dark my dog found it among the bushes. The owner over the house had in the meantime retired with his hands to his ears.

8. Wednesfield Schools

The first school was built in New Street in 1837 on land given by Richard Fryer. The building was in use until the opening of the National School in Graiseley Lane in 1856. New Street School was demolished in the 1920's. National Schools (mixed) Graiseley Lane erected in 1856 for 285 boys and girls and 115 infants; average attendance 260 boys and girls and 140 infants: Peter E Fanshaw, headmaster; Miss Mary Ann Corbett, infant's headmistress. The school consisted of a large room divided by a partition; two classrooms, porches and a separate infants department.

In 1863 when the log books first commenced, the master was Mr Thomas Cutting – Webb, class two certificates, Mrs Webb, who took the girls for sewing and Miss Knight, mistress of the girl's school. The building was lit originally by oil lamps because on September 20th 1864 there was an entry in the book stating that gas was being laid in the school (those pesky chickens). Heating was by coal fires in open grates, fires were rarely lit before December 1st and were finished with by April, unless the children came in soaked with rain, when an out of season fire was lit to dry their clothes.

Fig.10. Wednesfield National School, Graiseley Lane built 1856.

Fig.11. School Masters House said by some to have been haunted.

Fig.12. St Thomas' Church School on the site of William Bentley Court.

Fig.12a. Church of England School: Photo taken from Hickman Street about 1965. Old houses on corner already demolished; that was Newey's old house.

Fig.14. Aerial view of Wednesfield Church of England School built 1931. McConkeys building just beyond school to the left. Old air raid shelter still there to the right of the car.

National, Wood End (mixed) opened 27th July 1875 for 150 children; average attendance, 135; Miss L Masters, Mistress.

Board, Neachells Lane erected in 1895 for 200 boys and girls and 100 infants; Fred Last, Master.

Fig.15. Wood End Infant School built in 1875

Wards Bridge County Secondary School

Wards Bridge County Secondary School opened on 4th September 1956. It became Wards Bridge High School, a comprehensive school in July 1969. It closed in July 1989 and the buidling became the Jennie Lee Professional (Teachers) Centre in 1990. Plans at the moment are to redevelop the site.

Danesmore Primary School

Kitchen Lane County Primary School opened in 1956. The school was renamed Danesfield Primary School in 1983. It merged with Ashmore Park Primary to become Danesmore Park.

Ashmore Park County Primary School

Situated in Russell Close and opened in April 1958. It merged with Danesmore Primary in 1983.

St Thomas CE Primary School

St Thomas Infant School opened in 1876 in Wood End Road. A new school opened in Mattox Road in 1965 combining the Juniors and Infants.

Perry Hall Infant and Junior School
Perry Hall School opened in September 1949 as a Primary School and was officially opened in March 1951. In September 1956 a separate Infant School was opened on an adjacent site. In April 1993 the two schools joined to become Perry Hall Primary School once again.

Wood End Junior School
The Junior School opened in September 1938, in 1954 the Infant and Junior departments merged to form Wood End Primary School.

Coppice High School
Coppice Secondary School, Ecclestone Road was built in 1966. In 1970 the school was renamed Coppice High School. Later it became Coppice Community High School.

D'eyncourt Primary School
The school opened in January 1962. It was built to ease the pressure on school places at Long Knowle Primary School.

Wednesfield Village Primary School
The school was formed around 1992 by the amalgamation of Neachells Infant and Chadsway Junior Schools. The school closed as a result of amalgamation December 31st 2007.

Wodensfield Infant and Junior School
The school was formerly Woden Avenue School, opened in April 1932. The name changed to Wodensfield around 1971 when separate Infant and Junior schools were formed. In 1990 the departments merged to form Wodensfield Primary School.

Wednesfield High School
The school was formerly Wednesfield Grammar School. It was established in 1950. In 1969 the grammar school was merged with March End Secondary Modern School to form Wednesfield High School.

March End Secondary School
The school opened in January 1962. That was one of the coldest winters we have ever encountered.

Moathouse Junior and Infants School
The school opened in 1951.

9. Orchard Buildings / Rickyard.

The Orchard Buildings was a small compact estate on open ground near to Church Bridge in Graiseley Lane.
The buildings ran right through to what is now called Duke Street. The buildings dated back to the mid-19th century and the estate consisted of about 37 houses.
The site was a hive of activity, there were small workshops at the back of some of the houses, and some made locks, another made chains, (McConkey's), toward the 1970's the site was used as a car dismantler yard.

Fig.16. McConkey's staff 1930's (chainmakers)

A group of chainmakers who worked at the Orchard Buildings, Graiseley Lane. Back row: (L-R) Bill McConkey, Mr Lathe, John McConkey, SidneyMcConkey, unknown. Second row: (L-R) Mavis Allcock, Mary Wapples, Mrs Vincent, Gladys Gray, Iris Turner. Front row: (L-R) Peggy Bough, Miss Winifred Leeding, Gloria Pallant, Miss Brown, Miss Brown, unknown, unknown.

Rickyard

You could cross over the canal via Barn Bridge to the land behind the Boat Inn, at that time you could reach the Rickyard directly from the bridge.

Fig.17. Rickyard 1939

View from Barn Bridge, demolished late 60's early 70's. We now have a new bridge there called Trap Makers Bridge. Those old houses on the Rickyard were proper old fashioned Wednesfield houses. Do you recall them?

10. Arkinstalls the Blacksmiths

Mr Richard Arkinstall was the Blacksmith in Long Knowle Lane opposite Sunny Days; five houses now stand on that site.

Fig.18. Arkinstalls Smithy 1940's. Later a petrol station stood on the site.

11. Ideal Cinema / Methodist Church Rookery

The building was at first a Methodist Church later to become a cinema (The Ideal Cinema or better known as the 'Smack'. After the Smack closed in the 1960's the building was later used as a carpet warehouse. Couple of things to note, the Gable end of the building had a square front, all three photos show this.

Fig.19. Trinity Methodist Church late 19th Century.

Fig.20. Ideal Cinema 1920's

Fig.21. Carpet Warehouse prior to the arsonist attack on Sunday evening November 11th 1990.

12. Welfare Foods Campaign in the Midland Region

Wednesfield Staffs 7th September 1950.

Mr Broomhall said he understood the reason for the meeting was the very low uptake of Welfare Foods in the Wednesfield District and he asked every mother at the meeting to encourage her friends and neighbours with young children to make a better use of this service. Among those at the meeting Mr S Broomhall (Chairman of the Food Control Committee) Nurse Riley (Health Visitor) and two well-known Wolverhampton footballers who added their advice on how to keep fit. They were Mr Bert Williams (England and Wolves Goalkeeper) and Mr Jimmy Dunn (Wolves outside right) who was accompanied by Mrs Dunn and 6 months old Phillip.

It just goes to show that Wednesfield was at one time deemed important enough to attract personalities from the football world who for their part; helped in every department where possible.

Fig.22. (Seated L-R) Mr Bert Williams, (England and Wolves goalkeeper), Mr Jimmy Dunn (Wolves inside right), Mrs Dunn and Mr S Broomhall (Chairman of the F.C.C)

Fig.23. Welfare Foods voluntary members.

These ladies look like they are ready to eat after a hard day's work. All voluntary of course and it must be said what a wonderful job these ladies made of promoting Welfare Foods. Do you recognise any of these wonderful women volunteers who worked so hard? Let's hope that they had a meal befitting a king.

12a. Wednesfield Park 1950's / Bowling Teams

The development of parks and recreation grounds was among the Councils improvement schemes.

The four acre park and recreation ground was laid out as long ago as 1925 and in 1936 a further fourteen acres adjoining was acquired. A fully equipped playing field for children had been completed and the rest of the land levelled, seeded and fenced. The site was called King George's Field.

Bowls; there were two bowling greens in the park with several others in the District.

Tennis; there were two hard courts and a pavilion in the park. A Tennis Club in connection with the Civil Defence Services had courts and a pavilion at the British Legion Club premises in Vicarage Road.

Fig.24. Paddling Pool opened 1939.

Is there anybody here that you may recognise? Could it be your mother or father paddling away as happy as a skylark.

Fig.25. Lilly pond in the Old Park / flower park 1950's.

The old park used to be a favourite haunt of the older generation of Wednesfield and also the odd courting couple.

Fig.26. Wednesfield Paddling Pool 1963; the pool was opened in 1939.

Fig.27. Allotments top of Duke Street by the park

Fig.28. New Crown Bowling Team: Bottom row: (L-R) R Oakley, F J Noble, A Saunders, Mrs R Oakley, S Goodyear, Mrs W Downing, B Beeston League Sec, B Smith, Ray Oakley. Middle row: W Powell, B Tomlinson, E George, J Guffogg, C Langley, S Littlehales, H Green, P Terry, Les Littlehales and C Terry. Top row: K Smith, H Palmer, O Hand, R Wood, R Littlehales and T Knoble.

President S Goodyear Esq, Vice Presidents Dr W Bentley, R Oakley Esq, B Beeston Esq, Mrs W Downing, A Saunders Esq, E Green Esq, Ray Oakley Esq, G Wall Esq, H Bate Esq, H G Beech Esq, J P G Hinton Esq, Mrs R Oakley, Captain B Smith, Chairman: Ray Oakley Esq, Hon Secretary: F J Noble.

Fig.29. This one is The Falcon bowling team sometime between 1915 and 1920. Do you recognise anyone?

Fig.30. Mr and Mrs J Gregory standing by the Dog and Partridge bowling green early 1900's, said to have been one of the finest greens in the Midlands.

Fig.31. The Dog and Partridge bowling team. Harry Gregory seated front row.

14. Wednesfield Social Club

This club was formed in 1936 by a group of business men and in 1953 had a membership of nearly 800, including women members. Amenities included: Snooker, Darts, Dominoes, Bowls and Crib, each section having a team for various leagues. A pianist was available at weekends and there was entertainment by a concert party in the big room each Sunday evening throughout the year. Members were allowed to bring visitors during the permitted hours.

All members and visitors had to obey club rules while on the premises.

The big room was used for all kinds of functions and during the Coronation the room, as well as outside was decorated with flags and coloured lights. On June 3rd 1953, the children of Bolton Road held their Coronation party in the club.

The chairman of the council at the time; Councillor Ratcliffe, Mr W C Morgan, clerk of the council and Councillor Bargery were present. The children received Coronation pencils and the third prize for the best decorated street was presented to the secretary by Councillor Ratcliffe.

Many people from Wednesfield used the Social Club. I was a committee member at one time, but though the club was popular in its time, its memberships started to dwindle until the club closed. You could take the kids there and have a game of bingo on a Saturday evening. The kids would sit with you eating crisps and drinking pop. Don't forget that it's not that long ago that kids were not allowed in pubs, so the clubs were a good thing because of being able to take the kids. Of course the rules changed and kids are now allowed into pubs to have a meal with their parents. That and other things have seen the decline of memberships in some clubs. Mind you, trade is not great at the moment for pubs. Just off the top of my head at this moment in time, the Pyle Cock is up for lease and so is the Angel. Times are changing so Bob used to sing. Yes they are certainly changing but are the changes for the best? No, not all of them, you don't need me to tell you that most things today are money orientated. If there is a profit in it, then change it. It does not matter who it effects as long as it lines their pockets.

15. Unknown Seven

It was only a four foot wide entry – dark and cheerless but it was the gateway to the outer world for the seven families who lived in court No.3 off the Wednesfield High Street

Hundreds of local folk must have passed the narrow entrance without realising that it led to seven little houses.

There were no back entrances to the houses; if the entry was somehow blocked, the siege of court No.3 would have been complete.

'Grandad' of the yard was Mr George Richards who celebrated his 80th birthday on November 10th 1954. He lived at No.7 with his 53 year old son George; they had lived there for 50 years.

At No.1 lived Mrs Hassall and her grand-daughter. Mrs Hassall had lived there for some 45 years.

No.2 was the home of another old age pensioner; Miss Roberts and Mrs Giles. Her grand-daughter and her 'hubby' lived at No.3. Mrs Giles lived there for over 41 years.

Mr and Mrs Williams and their child lived at No.4 and Mr and Mrs Blunt lived at No.5. Last but not least were Mr and Mrs Harries and their two children at No.6.

Court No.3 off the High Street was scheduled for demolishment prior to housing development in 1954/5. While recognising that housing progress was inevitable and that they would be the last to stand in its way, the folk of No.3 had but one wish. It was when they had to go, they hoped the council would not send them too far away from the High Street as the familiar passing scene had become an integral part of their lives. Well, where was No.3 court just off the High Street? And where did those families move to?

16. Opening ceremony of the first house on the Long Knowle housing estate.

On Tuesday afternoon on the 8th September 1953, in glorious sunshine and in the presence of a representative gathering including members and officials of neighbouring local authorities. The first house on this estate was officially opened by Alderman Wm Neville OBE.

The function commenced with prayers offered by the chairman's chaplain, the Rev HW Marratt and the chairman of the Wednesfield Council, Councillor W G Ratcliffe, welcomed the visitors. He referred to the successful efforts of his council to meet their obligations under the 'overspill' agreement and gave facts and figures about the developments.
The overspill scheme began in March 1952 and 1955 would see the completion of the Long Knowle Estate and in that year of 1955, the first houses on the other overspill estate Ashmore Park were handed over.
Obviously lots of people live on these two estates. They were built because of the shortage of houses for Wednesfield's residents. Let's not forget that Ashmore Park was all fields prior to the estate being built and if my memory is correct, open cast mining was done on that land, for Long Knowle, fields again but with a few private houses and farms. It seems like Long Knowle has always been there. Don't forget that if you live on Ashmore Park or Long Knowle you are the overspill estates for Wednesfield.
In 1956 there was a ceremony to commemorate the 1000th house built on Ashmore Park; the house was 100 Kitchen Lane.

17. Sea Cadet Corps 1953

Wednesfield boys who were members of the Wolverhampton Sea Cadets had a very busy time during August, both at the 'ship' in Springfield Road and in Naval establishments.
Some twenty two cadets had been away on courses in HM ships and Establishments, among them being the following Wednesfield boys: Able Seaman K Bailey of 21 Lawfred Avenue who spent a fortnight in HMS Sea Eagle, Londonderry; the NATO Anti-Submarine Training School, and R Boycott and W Chester of Lawfred Avenue and E and C Taylor of Prestwood Road, all of whom were at HMS Ganges, the training establishment at Shotley, near Harwich.
Those who remained behind were also well catered for. The minature Naval Base at Lake Belvide, maintained by the Wolverhampton Unit Sea Cadets was continually open for practical boat work under sail and oar, while those interested in power boats had trips in the

pinnace on the Severn at Worcester under the direction of Lieut W Phipps, RNVR.
The summer saw the opportunities of cruising on inland waterways. Sea Cadets formed part of the crew of the ERNEST THOMAS barge, the Wolverhampton Youth Organisations barge, on a trip to London during August; the Sea Cadets had the barge themselves for a weekend cruise on the Shropshire Union Canal.
The barge, power driven had sleeping accommodation for 24 and good cooking facilities.
Wednesfield boys were made aware that owing to a number of sea cadets having been taken up for National Service in the Royal Navy and the Merchant Service, there were a few vacancies for keen boys of 15 and under who were anxious to do their National Service at sea. Practical seamanship in boats under sail and oar and power, signalling visual and wireless, rifle shooting, first aid and air training instruction were all available.
Candidates had to apply at once to Lt Commander F K Turner, Sea Cadet HQ, and Springfield Road. Were you in the sea cadets?

18. Wednesfield girls celebrate their 21st birthdays 1953

Several Wednesfield girls celebrated their twenty first birthdays, among them Muriel Price of 46 Bolton Road; Pearl Simmons of 32 Bolton Road and Beryl Jones of 20 Bolton Road. Many happy returns to you all and all good wishes for the future.
On September 19th Mrs Cull celebrated her ninety second birthday with a party for about fifty relatives and friends in the Conservative Club, Neachells Lane. We wish Mrs Cull a very happy birthday.
The wedding took place on August 29th at St Stephens Church between Mr George Burgess and Miss Gertrude Shaw of 66 Carlton Avenue.
Another wedding that took place at 2 o clock on September 5th at St Thomas' Church was that between Iris; daughter of Mr and Mrs W Nicholls of 45 Hickman Street and Frank, eldest son of Mr and Mrs Matthews of 100 First Avenue, Low Hill.

Pause for thought.
We plough the fields and scatter; the good seed on the land, but it is fed and watered by God's almighty hand.
How we enjoy singing those delightful harvest hymns that forcibly bring to our notice our inability to accomplish anything without the good hand of God upon us.
The seed is grown in the glorious hope of harvest. We tend and care for the struggling plant, but God first gives it life and having given life sustains it by weather changes to yield forth its fruit in due season. Paul said "I live, yet not I, but Chrust liveth in me." The seed of the abundant life had sown in Paul's heart and he lived in the knowledge of Christ's own utterance, I have come that ye might have life and that ye might have it more abundantly. "Only a reed shaken in the wind, but put in its place it becomes an organ note."

19. Golden / local Weddings / Birthdays

Birthdays

Birthday greetings to Mrs Polly Wallbank of 44 Lichfield Road and late of Orchard Buildings who was 87 on September 10th. Mrs Wallbank enjoyed having her half hour in the Cross Guns Inn every week with her family.
Birthday greetings to Mrs Sarah Lathan of 94 Victoria Road who was 80 on September 11th.
Birthday greetings also to Mrs Betty Clark of 45 Well Lane who attained her majority on September 25th.
Greetings go also to Veronica Timmis of 33 Bolton Road who was 2 years on September 11th; also Cynthia Round 64 Bolton Road who was 2 years on September 13th.
Greetings go also to John Fletcher 63 Linthouse Avenue who was 12 on October 11th.
Happy Birthday greetings also to Mr John Burgess of 50 Bolton Road who was 80 years on October 15th. Mr Burgess was born in Taylor Street and has lived in Wednesfield all his life.
Congratulations to Mr and Mrs T Phillips of 13 Graiseley Lane who celebrated their Golden Wedding on April 4th. They were married at Union Street, Willenhall in 1904 and had resided in Wednesfield for

many years. Mr Phillips was 73 years of age and his wife was 70. Birthday greetings go to Mrs Norwood who was living with her daughter Mrs Crochett at 74 Bolton Road. Mrs Norwood was 92 on April 2nd. She has five daughters and two sons, seven grandchildren and eight great grandchildren.

Local Weddings

The wedding took place at St Thomas' Church on Saturday September 11th of Mr John Thomas Turner of Bilston and Miss Olive Price, eldest daughter of Mr and Mrs Jim Price of 4 Highfield Crescent. The bride wore blue taffeta with a white lace. The best man was Mr Robert Turner brother of the bridegroom.

The reception was held at the Church Institute and the honeymoon spent at Paignton.

On September 18th at St Thomas' Church, Mr R Evans of 54 Neachells Lane was married to Miss Iris Smith, daughter of Mr and Mrs Harry Smith of 118 Wood End Road. The bride carried a white prayer book and pink roses and her bridesmaid Miss Betty Footman carried a prayer book and white carnations.

The reception was held at the Church Institute and afterwards the bridal couple left for a honeymoon in London.

The wedding also took place at St Thomas Church on September 18th between Mr L D Cox of 7 Park House Avenue, son of Mrs Mary Cox and the late Mr Thomas Cox, and Miss Andre Patricia Venville; youngest daughter of Mr and Mrs W H Venville of 'Firndale' Vicarage Road. The bride wore silver brocade and carried pink roses and was attended by Miss Roma Venville, Miss Jean Cox and Miss Susan Venville. The best man was Mr Allan Cox. The reception was held at the New Crown Hotel and the honeymoon at Paignton.

Mr Arthur Harold Evans son of Mr G H Evans and the late Mrs Evans of Victoria Road, and Miss Constance Ethel Ball, daughter of the late Mr and Mrs F H Ball of Wolverhampton, were married on September 20th at Wimbourne Road Methodist Church, Fallings Park, Wolverhampton.

The bride, given away by her brother-in-law Mr Frederick Harding was attended by Miss Jean Evans, sister of the bridegroom and Miss

Shirley Cook, Mr Maurice Coleman was best man. A reception was held at the Newbridge Hotel, Tettenhall Road and later the bride and bridegroom left for their honeymoon to be spent in London.
The wedding took place at St Thomas Church recently between Mr Bernard Johnson, son of Mr and Mrs C F I Johnson of Moathouse Lane and Miss Dorothy May Lewis, daughter of Mrs N Lewis and the late Mr T Lewis of Wood End Road. The bride, who was given away by her uncle, wore a dress of white tulle over satin and was attended by four bridesmaids and one pageboy. The honeymoon was spent in Llandudno.
Mr Kenneth Simmons, son of Mr and Mrs Robert Simmons of 285 Wood End Road was married Saturday September 25th to Miss Irene Jones of Dunstall Road, Wolverhampton at St Thomas' Church. She was attended by Miss Beryl Simmons and Miss Rosemary Simmons and the best man was Mr Alfred Simmons.
Also on Saturday September 25th at St Thomas Church, the wedding took place between Mr Dennis Percival son of Mr and Mrs Arthur Percival of 23 Colman Avenue and Miss Eileen Turner, daughter of Mr and Mrs Thomas Henry Turner of 2 Moathouse Lane. She wore white net over figured satin and was attended by her two sisters and as sister of the bridegroom. The best man was Mr Fred Percival brother of the bridegroom. A reception was held at the Wednesfield Social Club.
It's great to look back at people's weddings and compare them to your own. They all sound great honeymoons; Paignton and London. It just makes you think of your own wedding. How did yours go? Don't forget that it's one of the three or four great things you will do in your lifetime. Okay what is the first? Well it's obvious; you are born so that's number 1. Number 2 must be when you get married; it's such a fantastic day, one that you will never forget. Okay lots of weddings are done on a budget for obvious reasons but at the end of the day a wedding is a wedding when you are in love. Number three must be for the majority of most people it's got to be you're first born. As a dad it has got to be the most fantastic feeling that you will ever have, even when you have sex, the feeling of being a dad is well, you know, so I need not put it into words; for words would be hard to find to

explain the feeling of being a dad to a new born son. You watch them grow up and you want them to achieve more than you ever have. The fourth; well I will let you guess at that.
While we are on the subject of weddings; where was your wedding held? If you got married in Wednesfield you probably got married in St Thomas' Church. Okay I know that there were other places in Wednesfield that you could get married at but all in all St Thomas' Church was the logical choice for most people. After all, I got married there.
It's marvellous that Kath can recall most things about our wedding day yet I can't; but to counter that I can recall our honeymoon only too well. Our honeymoon was spent on a barge on the canal in March of 1976. You have to admit that was a great choice of honeymoon destination. It snowed and rained and the boat broke down in Wheaton Aston. We decided that we'd had enough and abandoned the boat to return home and settle into married life where we could cuddle up and keep each other warm. Something that was not possible on that cold barge; but having said all that it's those sorts of memories that will stay with you for the rest of your lives. I will say this about our honeymoon and that is that it's the coldest that I have ever been. Let's not forget that I have worked at Wolverhampton Racecourse and a certain chap called Mark Twain once said that the coldest winter's day he had ever encountered was a summer's day at Wolverhampton Racecourse. Well our honeymoon was colder than that but we can now look back and think yes it was cold but we are still here now. That means we must have paid our gas bill of £300 or more but hey we are not despondent because most people are in the same boat.

Golden Weddings
Well-known figures in Wood End; Mr and Mrs William Griffiths celebrated their golden wedding on September 4th. They were married by the Rev Guy Parkhouse at St Thomas' Church, Wednesfield 1904. Mr Griffiths now 73 years of age was the sole surviving son of the late Mr and Mrs Thomas Griffiths, who was in his younger days very active, playing football for Willenhall Pickwicks.

Mrs Griffiths was born in Heath Town 70 years ago. She can recall when she sold loaves of bread at 4lb for 3 ½ d. There is one grandson. Congratulations on a great achievement.
Mr and Mrs J H Green of Victoria Road celebrated their Golden Wedding on Friday September 17th. Both Mr and Mrs Green are 75 years of age. They have one son, one daughter and seven grandchildren. Congratulations all round on a great achievement.

20. Local Trades 1954/5

Looking at a 1954/5 official guide for Wednesfield, Staffordshire; the first thing that caught my eye was the Urban District Council badge that's on the front cover. It's the exact same badge or crest that the Wednesfield Heritage Society has adopted. The booklet has a list of local companies that advertised in there. I will give you a few examples. I am sure that you have heard of most if not all of those advertised in the guide.
First we have Squire's Hardware Stores of Rookery Street, Draper and Ward Manufacturers and Designers of Perrit Bars for the enamelling trade Empire Works, High Street. Wilfred Russell and Co again Perrit Bars for the enamelling trade, again; same address Empire Works, High Street. what are Perrit Bars, does anybody know? White and Poole (Engineers) Ltd all types of machining and light and medium pressings. A E Jenks and Cattell Ltd, Phoenix Works, Neachells Lane makers of pressings in all trades. Light garden tools including rakes, forks, hoes and trowels etc... Gates and grids for gas cookers, door bolts – gate latches, hearth furniture and scraper mats.
Abraham Pursehouse and Sons Public Works and Building Contractors, Rookery Street.
H Ellard Waddensbrook Estate Engineers Press workers manufacturers of parts for gas, electric cookers and refridgeraters, plate racks, wire shelves, grill pans and oven pans.
J Shelton; Stationer, 8 High Street.
W G Ralphs and Son; Metal and Wood pattern makers, Wolverhampton Road.
The Unit Electrical Instillation Co; every type of installation or repairs, lighting, heating and radio repairs, 3 High Street.

John and Joseph Goodare Ltd manufacturers of hooks and hinges, spout brackets etc...Rookery works.
S E Foster Transport Contractor, Hall Street. Joseph Foulkes Ltd House and Industrial Fuel Road and Canal Transport, Victoria Wharf. The 'Wodensfield Press' proprietor: E Mattox, 7 High Street.
The IDEC ELECTRIC Electrical Installations, 11 Rookery Street. The Doran Engineering Co Ltd; high class bright bolts and nuts, New Street.
J T Dancer established 1850 manufacturer of mortise, rim, asylum, prison and ship locks and all kind of keys, Hall Street.
The Falcon Engineering Co, auto and lock components etc...Hart Road.
The Wolverhampton Metal Co Ltd non – ferrous metal refiners and smelters on admiralty, war office and AID lists, Well Lane.
The Wednesfield Motor and Cycle garage all makes of cars and motorcycles supplied Wolverhampton Road. Robert Harris Ltd, Waddensbrook Estate Presswork and Welding, also lock and latch manufacturers. Clay's builders and contractors, New Street.
That's a good list of companies that were around in the 1950's. You are sure to recall some of them; you may have even worked at some of them. There are just a few more for you to recall.
D H Woods Phillips, Norman and Eagle Cycles also complete Anglers outfits, 13 Rookery Street. Did you ever go there for some fishing tackle? Or a bike?
W P Pickering Newsagents, 2 High Street.
S R Bayley, 33 High Street, grocer provision and corn merchant; finally the Pheasant Stores grocery and provisions Wood End Road.

21. 1950's

Attainment July

We bring to the front; eight year old Stephen Sanders of 39 South Avenue. For some weeks now, Steve has been walking about on crutches after fracturing his leg playing football in the park.
Steve admits that he cried a bit when it happened, but after having his leg x-rayed and encased in plaster at the Royal Hospital and spending a fortnight off school, he quickly resumed his health and spirits. It is a

tonic to see one so young adapting himself so bravely and cheerfully to an unfortunate and temporary handicap.
Mr and Mrs Sanders can be proud of their son and although Mrs Sanders fetches Steve from school with her bicycle, we feel sure Stephen will soon be throwing those crutches away.
His brother Tommy, 21, spent his holiday on the Isle of Wight. Steve's birthday is on Christmas Eve; he will be glad to forget when he was eight.

Mr George Watts 1955

One of the most genial personalities of the older brigade living in Wednesfield was George Watts who resided at 2 Woden Way and was 82 years of age in 1955. His life had been most busy and varied, a brief account follows.
George Watts started work at the age of eight delivering bread for his father who was a baker in Birmingham. He was later apprenticed to a confectioner and at the age of 23 commenced business on his own account in the well-known Horse Fair at Bristol Road, Birmingham. He subsequently joined the Queens own Worcestershire regiment (during which time he won first prize for sword butting) and afterwards the Staffordshire Yeomanry for 7 years for which he was principle caterer.
In 1910 he went to work at Hickman's Steel Works at Bilston where he resided for 12 years then moving to Wednesfield where he was caterer for the Weldless Steel Tube Canteen.
His proudest memories of this time were dealing with the catering for the Annual Wednesfield Comforts Fund-the old people's supper, having the assistance of butchers Hulme, Hill and Downing. What feasts they were! Five rounds of beef and two barrels of beer of the quality about which he now dreams.
Mr Watts's next move was to take charge of the confectioners and outdoor beer license in North Street where he stayed for 25 years.
Since his retirement George has been connected with the Sons of Rest of which he was one of the first members, and together with his wife were members of the friendship club.

George and his wife have been living in one of the old people's bungalows Woden Way for the last 5 years and there are none more appreciative of the comfort of these bungalows than Mr and Mrs Watts.

May God spare them quite a few more years yet to enjoy their well-earned retirement.

Sons of Rest Pavillion

The brick built hall was situated in the park adjacent to the tennis courts. It was erected by public subscription in 1947 to provide comfort for elderly men. The hall was centrally heated and had a kitchenette and was provided with chairs and tables of tubular steel. Many of the patrons that used the hall were in their eighties, which gave convincing evidence of the hardiness of Wednesfield people.

Fig.32. Interior of the Sons of Rest Pavllion.

General Information

Banks; Barclays, 47 High Street; Trustees Savings Bank, 7 High Street.
Births, Marriages; Registrar J H Turley, Regent Buildings, Hall Street Bilston. The registrar was in attendance at the Church Institute, Graiseley Lane on Wednesdays from 2.30pm – 5.00pm.

Church Yard; Graiseley Lane and Cemetary Road.
Citizens Advice Bureau; Secretary Mrs D E Bellamy, 100 Prestwood Road West.
Civic Restaurant; Well Lane. Hours of opening: 12 noon to 2.30pm Monday to Friday. Early closing day – Thursday.
Licensing Hours; 12 noon to 2pm; 6pm to 10pm.
Local Newspapers; Express and Star daily pm 1 ½ d; office 50 Queen Street, Wolverhampton. Wolverhampton Chronicle, Friday 2d.
Police Stations; Wolverhampton Road (Tel 31230), Wood End (Tel 31211).
Soil Light; Subsoil, coal and iron.
Telephone Kiosks; Kiosks were to be found in the following locations: High Street, Graiseley Lane, Lichfield Road, The Scotlands, Broad Lane, Stubby Lane, Wood End and Mill Lane.
Territorial Army; Headquarters were at the Drill Hall, Lichfield Road.

The U.D.C'S Gala Day

The bunting, flags and decoratives were in view on April 2nd 1955 as Wednesfield at last opened its long sought after council offices.
The occasion was celebrated by a luncheon in the Royal Oak Hotel which fully appreciated both the gravity and the joy of the occasion. The menu certainly served to whet the appetite of the diners and the after lunch speakers explained why. Grace was spoken by the Rev C D Johnson and after a splendid meal, Her Majesty the Queen was royally toasted. Proposing the health of the guests, the Chairman of the council, Mr G E Higgs, J P mentioned the threat of Wednesfield's independence that the Staffs County merging proposals made. He was glad therefore to welcome the guests on such a noteworthy occasion when full ministry approval had sanctioned the building of the offices and indicated some measure of confidence in Wednesfield's abilities. He paid tribute to all present, which in various ways had helped to put forward the erection of the offices and was pleased that so many guests had been able to come.
The response for the guests was made by the divisional M P , Miss Jennie Lee, who relieved at the easing of her noted husband's career said "I am pleased that in these days when most people use bricks to

throw, the council have put bricks to their rightful purpose, to build up". She thanked the council for their invitations and wished Wednesfield long independence and great success in all spheres.
Mr W A Wood, the principal regional officer proposed the toast to the urban district of Wednesfield. He said that he arrived in the Midland region a year and a day ago (April 1st!) He hoped that there was nothing ominous in that. He was glad to celebrate the occasion with Wednesfield U.D.C! He had found the Midlands region most friendly and its authorities helpful and it seemed to him that there was much to be said for the fine civic spirit and careful planning such authorities exhibited. He wished Wednesfield well! According to Councillor Haden there was a tremendous independent spirit in Wednesfield and it would be hard lines for any authority that failed to see this and refused to keep away.

Opening Time

There followed at 3pm, the official opening of the new offices in Regal Fields. The weather became overcast and with rain falling strongly, the ceremony had to be held indoors. Many visitors thronged the corridors tightly packing the main entrance.
The Chairman of the Council, Mr George Higgs J P opened the proceedings and heartily welcomed the visitors to a memorable and happy occasion. He declared that these offices would serve always a useful purpose and greatly assist the efficiency of the council.
He stressed that although they had not been allowed to build a council – chamber he hoped this would yet be possible. The offices were but the first part of a permanent scheme to build a Public Health Centre and Civic Hall around the offices making the whole a real town centre. Mr A Wood then formally opened the offices. He received the presentation key provided by the architects, Messrs Cleland and Hayward and in his speech stated his pleasure in coming. Mr Wood was most discrete in his remarks and gave no hint as to the eventual outcome of the merging proposals of the county which thoughts were uppermost in the minds of those assembled.
The Rev H Baylis, M A, C F then conducted prayers of blessing for the rightful use of the new buildings. There followed the unveiling of the

memorial bust of the late Mr David Pritchard, J P, who had been chairman of the council from 1925 to 1931. Sir Geoffrey Mander performed the unveiling and paid high tribute to the sterling qualities both of character and civic initiative that David Pritchard exhibited. He said that Mr Pritchard's whole life was wrapped up with the welfare of his native Wednesfield. It was good to note that his wife, Mrs E .N Pritchard and David, their son were present. Councillors James and guest thanked Mr Wood for opening the offices and Councillors Broomhall and Bird expressed gratitude to Sir Geoffrey Mander. There followed a most delightful tour of Wednesfield's new civic pride – her council offices and an excellent buffet tea ended the days celebrations.

You're Representatives – A brief outline of Members of Wednesfield UDC 1955.

Mrs Mary Newey J P

Mrs Newey entered the council in 1946 as she was the only woman councillor – one woman amongst the men. Mrs Newey was not perturbed at being outnumbered and made her points briskly and authoritively in open council meetings. She served on six council committees, being Vice Chairman of the Public Health Committee. She served on the Area Health Committee and was a governor of the Evening Institute and a teacher at Beacon C P School where she was chief assistant. Also, Mrs Newey was a J P in the Tettenhall Division. Being a housewife and mother of three children, Sheila, Trevor and Phillip; her husband was Mr A J Newey. When she had the time, Mrs Newey liked to read, and her keen interest centered on local history; she was also adept at elocution and speech training. The Neweys lived in Lichfield Road, Mrs Newey in Wednesbury before coming to Wednesfield.

Mr Abel Guest

Mr Guest was the father of the council, having the longest serving record of any of the members, in all 35 years, truly a lifetime in public affairs. He has been U.D.C Chairman five times and served on innumerable committees. Mr and Mrs Guest came from Bromsgrove,

Worcs, to Wednesfield where Mr Guest set up a market gardening business around the turn of the century. Their family settled in this area and their grandchildren gave them much happiness. The Guests lived in Wood End Road; Mr Guest was an independent member of that ward on the council. Mr Guest was Chairman of several council committees. He represented the U.D.C on the joint Industrial Council. His educational interests extended further for he was Chairman of the managers of Wood End Road and Moathouse Lane Schools and a governor of St Thomas' and Lichfield Road Schools.
Mr Guest was a member of Hickman Street Methodist Church and was a most acceptable local preacher in Methodist Churches and was a well-known and respected figure throughout the area.

Mr Stanley Broomhall

There can be fewer district figures better known than Mr Stan Broomhall for he was Wednesfield's Postmaster and having been in public life for eighteen years with its attendant activities he was familiar to most Wednesfield folk, friendly to all and has been helpful to not a few.

Fig.33. Stanley Broomhall; your representative.

Mr Broomhall's political affiliation was conservative. As founder – president of the Wednesfield Horticultural Society, it folllowed that Mr Broomhall was keen on gardening; which he did when he had the time. During the war Mrs Broomhall was a Senior Warden in Civil Defence.
He was very much a family man; his wife Mrs Julia Broomhall ran a drapery

business in the Post Office with charm and ability and so at last saw something of her husband by day if not in the evening. The Broomhalls lived in Vicarage Road; they had two sons Peter and Norman and three daughters Margaret, Rosalind and Gillian.

Mr Harry M Griffiths

A native of Wednesfield; a building contractor who ran the family business, and a councillor who served continuously since 1934; Mr Griffiths was a man with a great range of activities and interests. He was twice Chairman of the U.D.C and was Chairman of the Housing and Town Planning Committee and was a member of nine committees in the council's interest. He had been Civil Defence Chairman, a governor of Bilston Girls High School, secretary of the local musical festival and a treasurer of the former P O W committee. He was a keen gardener and also a keen supporter of Wolves, rarely missing a match. His wife Mrs Evelyn Griffiths was also well known in the district and their family consisted of Alan, Brian and Diana. They all lived in Woodgate, Amos Lane.

Mr George E Higgs, J P

Mr Higgs was the Chairman of Wednesfield U.D.C in 1955. A most capable and modest man, Mr Higgs was associated with the labour Party for many years and was Labour representation on the council. He was chief inspector with the Willenhall firm of John Harper and Co and was himself a Willenhall man. Councillor Higg's wife, Mrs Margaret Higgs came from Stourbridge and she was a school teacher at Perry Hall School. She gained her teaching diploma at Dudley Training College. She supported her husband actively in all his work. They have a 12 year old daughter, Margaret Anne who attended the Girls High School in Wolverhampton. The Higgs lived at 195 Lichfield Road.

Hey Ho! Come to the fair!
Frolic Day – July 2nd 1955

July 2nd was an important day in the life of Wednesfield: it was carnival day in Wednesfield and 20,000 people were expected to assemble on the King George playing fields to join in the fun and watch the attractions; for attractions and fun were provided in plenty. Admission was one shilling for adults and sixpence for children. From 1.45pm in the afternoon entrance was allowed and at 2pm, the tableaux and competitors for judging assembled; judging began at 2.15pm.

The Carnival Queen

Miss Rita Terry, a well-known and well liked local girl of nineteen summers was chosen as the Carnival Queen. She lived in Lewis Grove, Wednesfield. Her four attendants who, like the Queen were dressed in white were: Wendy Felton of 16 Nordley Road, Patricia Tasker of 27 Moat Green Avenue, Christine Brooks of 99 Cadman Crescent and Cynthia Jones of Wood End Road, Wednesfield. The King of Mirth who no doubt caused many surprises on the day was Mr Jack Leighton of 210 Wood End Road. He proved an acceptable monarch. The Prime Minister was Mr Ray Parker of Cherry Grove. They succeeded for their talents were many. John Fletcher of 63 Olinthus Avenue was the Queen's herald.

Procession Started

The official opening by the Chairman of the local council, Mr C T Squire was timed at 2.45pm and at 3pm the programme began. The procession got underway for its tour of Wednesfield, lasting one hour to entice any reluctant visitors to hasten to the carnival grounds. From 3.15pm til 9pm the carnival pursued its merry way. Continuous attractions proceeded throughout that time. The Tunstall Girls College gave their famous musical horse rides and there was a demonstration of trained dogs by the Walsall Alsatian Society. There was a Mass Band Display from six bands and a jazz competition with money prizes for the winners.

Further Attractions

A grand variety show was given by the Wolverhampton and District Entertainments Club there were exhibitors of national folk dancing by Polish and Ukrainian national dancers. The Wednesfield Male Voice

Choir under Mr Alfred Pugh also entertained with their fine part singing.
Considerable interest was shown in the tug of wars being arranged by the Wednesfield Indoor Sports League. Small boys in particular gazed with awe struck faces of muscular contortions and everyone else gathered to laugh and cheer. A balloon race was a novelty in itself and a must for children. One of the more intriguing and highly dangerous displays was the display of scientific judo or jujitsu by the Wulfruna Judo Society. Many flocked to see this. There was a prize of 10 shillings to the finder of the needle in the haystack; one of the many competitions for folk to join in.

Babies on view
Of supreme interest every year was the baby's show, which was arranged by the Toc H ladies. It was for all the baby's up to 36 months old and Wednesfield no doubt saw its future dominant citizens behave themselves. Babies have a habit of stealing the limelight; all days are alike to them, if not to their mothers, but they did enjoy the Punch and Judy show with Punch and the crocodile fighting it out. There was a continuous flow of refreshments, with lemonade and ice cream as the favourites. Licensed refreshments were also available. Pony and donkey rides were given for amusement, roundabouts, dodgems and swing boats had their appeal. The Toc H men arranged other sideshows.

Fig. 34. August 1956 baby show. Mothers holding their babies.

THE BEST EVER

When pressed for his last minute comments about the carnival, the chairman of the committee Mr N A Purshous declared that this carnival was planned to be better than ever. "If the weather gives us a good break it will be a better show than last year and very worthwhile seeing it: it is undoubtedly one of the best in the Midlands," he declared. How's about that then? One of the best carnivals in the Midlands, so where is Wednesfield Carnival today?
Profits from the carnival were for local charities; about £1,200 was raised on the day. When expenses were deducted from this; it was hoped to have the largest ever donation amounts for division among listed organisations. There was no doubt about it; Wednesfield went to town on July 2nd 1955, or rather to the fair.

Carnival Courage

Hats off to Mrs Minnie Harvey of East Avenue and Mrs Daisey Freeman of Lewis Grove who were responsible for the refreshments in Wednesfield's charity making carnival. So as to cut down all expense and make as much profit as they could to give needy organisations, these two ladies delayed necessary vegetables until the evening before when the prices of tomatoes and cucumbers etc...were a penny or two less. This meant added work for everything had to be done at once but it was saving a penny. Sadly however, it pounded down and the two womenfolk tottering under their heavy burdens were badly drenched and soaked.

Wednesfield Library Opening

Wednesfield's new branch library was well and truly opened on May 14th 1955 and the crowd who gathered were eager to do business straightaway. The library which cost about £5000 is 60 foot by 25 foot, flat roofed and prefabricated. It is the third building of its sort to be erected by the county.
Miss Jennie Lee, M P performed the opening ceremony. As a holder of two degrees and a student of literature; Miss Lee was a most fitting opener. She listed the delights in store for all users of the library. They could go far beyond the bounds of Wednesfield through the medium

of books and all ages could unlock their secrets to them. TV, radio, stage and cinema were all inferior to the pleasure of a good book.
Mr H Gadsby as Chairman of the local library committee introduced the speakers who included Councillor G E Higgs and Ald Bayliss, Vice Chairman of the County Committee. Mr Gadsby stated that Wednesfield had been the longest single authority and he was glad that this moment had come. It was a milestone in Wednesfield's history. The library is open every day and since its opening has done a roaring trade particularly among children.
There were 11,000 books for librarian Mr W E Wilkes and his staff to look after. Well done back then to Mr Wilkes and his staff, how many books do you think are in today's library compared to 1955? Well things have changed a bit since 1955, some 56 years ago. Now we have computers and people can access more information than they could ever do in the past.

Fig. 35. The old library.

Wednesfield folks birthdays

Birthday greetings to Thomas Lovatt, of 7 Tithe Road who on July 14th 1955 was 79. Best wishes from his wife; Mr and Mrs Lovatt were very active and keen members of the Darby and Joan club.

Mr Ashbourne of 46 Neachells Lane, who on October 25th was 65. From someone who likes to remember, someone too nice to forget. From daughter Hilda and Henry and Grandsons Henry and Gordon; may God grant you many more birthdays in the years to come.
Carol Benton, 37 Neachells Lane; love from Mom, Dad, Gran and Uncle Albert.
Rock birthday greetings to dearest Mother on her 80th birthday on June 3rd 1955. Love and best wishes from daughter May, Frank and Grandchildren.
Rock happy birthday to Valerie on May 30th from Gran and Grandpa. 28 Lawrence Avenue.
Taylor- Birthday greetings and best wishes to the 'twins' of 2 Ridge Lane; Lilly and May who reached their 18th birthday on May 26th.
Mattox; Gran and Grandad send their best wishes to Valerie of 63 Neachells Lane who was 15 on June 5th.
Trubshaw- Greetings and good wishes to both Rosemary and Dorothy who, on April 6th were four. Happy birthday to each of you from Grandpa and Grandma Marshall.
Trevor- Greetings also to Dorothy on her 15th birthday on April 6th. Love and best wishes on your birthday from Mrs Bowdler and family.
Perry- Happy greetings to Pearl on her 14th birthday -31 East Avenue, Nordley Hill. Good luck Pearl.
Harries- Happy greetings to Roger of 62 Moathouse Lane who was 10 on April 11th.
Jennings- Birthday greetings to Josephine of 90 Bealeys Avenue who was 10 on April 1st. Many happy returns to you on your birthday.

Congratulations

Mr and Mrs H Broom of 77 Hart Road, Mr Broom was 81 years of age on 23rd August and Mrs Broom was 8o years of age on 20th August 1955. Mr and Mrs Broom, both natives of Willenhall were married in 1893 and moved to Wednesfield at the time when Hart Road was being developed. When the houses in Hart Road were built they moved into No.77 and had lived there for the past 45 years, of their family of seven sons, six were still very much alive, are married and

reside locally. There were fifteen grandchildren and two great grandchildren, who at the time were in Australia.
On March 9th 1955 Mr and Mrs Rogers of 30 Bolton Road celebrated the 59th anniversary of their wedding, a splendid achievement. Mr Rogers celebrated his 82nd birthday in April, Mrs Rogers had not been very well for some time but was getting better. To them both, best wishes.

Golden Wedding
Mr and Mrs Arthur L Durnall celebrated their golden wedding on Saturday April 22nd 1955. They had two married daughters and one grandchild. The Durnalls were married at St Stephens Church, Smethwick on April 22nd 1905 and came to live in Wednesfield at 68 Neachells Lane the same year; and have lived there ever since. Chairman of the Old People's Friendship Club Management Committee and a founder member of the Sons of Rest; Mr Arthur Durnall was amongst the most popular of Wednesfield's seniors. Born in 1880 at Bradley, Bilston, Mr Durnall commenced his working life at the age of 12 in the grocery trade. He later moved to Stretton, Stafford, where his father was licensee at the Bell Inn. Here he was employed as a farm worker. Later still he moved to Smethwick, Birmingham and worked at the British Tube Company's factory as a tube drawer. Finally in 1905, he came to Wednesfield to work at the Weldless Steel Tube Co, where he was employed for 32 years until his retirement in about 1947. Whilst employed at Smethwick, Arthur met his wife, a very charming personality indeed! They were married in 1905. Mr Durnall was an accomplished pianist and had acted on numerous occasions as 'minstrel' for the Buffs. He played at the friendship club meetings as well as being their Chairman. Arthur was an enthusiastic gardener and supplied his wife with most of their vegetable requirements; they were a lovely old couple.

Silver Wedding
Mr and Mrs H Spear of 32 Prestwood Avenue celebrated their silver wedding anniversary on July 9th 1955 we give them our heartiest congratulations and good wishes.

Old world cottages

These three old world cottages were situated adjacent to the Doran Engineering Company, March End Road, Wednesfield, disappeared from the Wednesfield scene in the early part of 1955 lying some 20 yards off the main road with spacious front grounds and hedges. Their picturesque frontal appearance belied their internal state. Nine residents had the use of one toilet, one wash house and had to walk some 10-15 yards for water and all of the drainings discharged into a cesspit some 20 feet in front of the grounds of the premises.
These same residents were then comfortably re-housed in new council houses and the cleared site was converted into a temporary car park by the adjacent manufacturing company.

Fig. 36. Old world cottages 1955

Snooker Supper

A very pleasant and successful night was held on Saturday 18th June 1955 when 40 members and guests of the snooker section sat down to their annual supper and prize distribution. After full justice had been done to a good meal the Chairman called on the club president, Councillor W H Bargery to present the prizes to George Jones the captain of the victorious team in the S. Staffs Billiards and Snooker Association and to the team; H Morby, F Morby, B Morby, I Brinsdon,

H Hollees and A Jordan their respective prizes and to the Captain; C Congreaves and team their prizes for winning the knock out section in the West Midlands. The secretary then had a pleasant surprise as the captain of the S. Staffs team produced a cup suitably inscribed and requested the president to present it to him for services rendered: a very nice gesture and much appreciated by the recipient! After the other cups and prizes had been awarded, the evening was bought to a close with a concert by the Variety Four to a packed concert room. There are some names that I am sure that most folk of Wednesfield will recognise; F Morby, could that be the Frank Morby of Well Lane, the well-known jockey? Wednesfield Social Club had photo's on their walls in the bar area showing Frank on various horses, where are these photo's now? Did you ever see them?

1956

Saturday 8th September 1956 at 3:00pm saw the official opening of the old people's welfare centre in Neachells Lane / Pickering Road (adjoining Pallants Garage) and to refreshments afterwards at the Council Offices, Alfred Squire Road. Secretary to the committee Mr J R Munslow, 54 Lichfield Avenue. Some facts regarding the centre:
The purpose of the centre is to operate various services to the aged folk of the district and to accommodate the existing 'Friendship Club'. The content price without fittings is £3,850. Towards this cost a grant of £1,250 has been obtained from the King George VI Memorial Fund, the second highest grant in the country. The site was sold to the committee by the Urban District Council for the nominal sum of £5. Flats for old people were to be erected by the council adjacent to the centre.
After the August monthly meeting of Wednesfield U.D.C the Chairman, Councillor C T Squire unveiled a board within the foyer of the council offices, commemorating the names of all those who had been Chairman of Council since Wednesfield authority was established in 1894. The unveiling was preceded by words from Councillors Squire and Ratcliffe, who referred to the growing progress of the Local Authority and remembered those who had played so notable a part in shaping district expansion. A dedicatory prayer was

given by the Chairman's Chaplain and refreshments followed in the Council Chamber at which many former Chairman of the Council and their relatives were present. Below was the list of names as they appeared on the board with their dates of office of the men who have been Wednesfield's 'chief citizens'.

1894-1902	Thomas Evans	1938-1939	Joseph Dudley
1903-1912	Enoch Hadley	1940-1941	William George Ratcliffe JP
1913-1918	William Sidebottom	1942-1943	Harry M Griffiths
1919	Enoch Hadley	1944-1945	Harold G Beech
1920	Richard H Lewis	1946-1947	Abel Guest
1921	Henry Clay	1948-1950	Clarence Haden
1922-1924	Abel Guest	1951-1952	Stanley Broomhall
1925-1931	David Pritchard JP	1953	William George Ratcliffe
1932-1933	William Davenport	1954	George E Higgs
1936-1937	Walter H Beard	1955-	Cyril T Squire JP

A measure of civic pride was truly reflected in this picture taken in the Council Offices foyer following the unveiling of the board of commemoration, there in which is contained the names of all who have been Chairmen of Wednesfield U.D.C.

Fig. 37. In the picture (L-R): H G Beech, Mr Clarence Haden, Cllr C T Squire JP, Cllr W G Ratcliffe JP, Mrs D E Squire, Mr J Henwood-Jones, Cllr S J Perks, Cllr G E Higgs, Mrs W M Perks.

Fig.38. Council Offices, Alfred Squire Road from site of Wednesfield Police Station 1959.

Retirement Pensioners

George Badger, living at 17 Wood Avenue had a very wide and varied experience in his 81 years of life. To list some of his many, many stories was really entertaining. George began working at the age of eleven following the plough and gathering up potatoes on the land on which now stands Nordley Hill Estate.

That's great because the estate was not built until 1920/21, so with George following the plough on that land is going back a bit; perhaps before your time as a reader. If it's not then you can have a free book from me with great pleasure, because if you were about 40 prior to 1920/21 then you would deserve a free book about Wednesfield Our Heritage. Anyway back to George, he toiled 10 hours a day and six days a week for which he was paid the princely sum of halfpenny an hour. In 1888 he commenced a job for the late Henry Clay, Sen, drawing coal from Holly Bank. Desiring a change, however, he then went to Pritchard's Ltd in Hickman Street as a tin trunk worker. The year 1889 took him to Lancashire to seek work. Residing with a relative somewhere in the county, he got a job delivering bread to the mill workers. After a while however, due to a dispute with his relatives he decided to move. Having very little money to spare for transport, he walked for 12 hours with four to six feet of snow on the ground into the neighbouring county of Yorkshire to again, change his job. Other occupations came the way of George Badger until he eventually settled down in 1906 as a collier at Ashmore Park and Holly Bank Collieries, where he worked until his retirement in 1946. Mr Badger lost his wife in 1947 and lived mostly alone since then. He cooked and (he said) felt much younger than his birth certificate revealed. Good luck for the future George.

W SNAPE AND SON (Tailors) Ltd

The notable front rank firm of tailors of Prince's Square Wolverhampton, was of Wednesfield origin and went from strength to strength here. It was founded in a small house in New Street about 1865 by Mr James Snape born in 1837, the year Queen Victoria was crowned. In 1874 he moved to the old Post Office, High Street, where Mr William Snape was born; then to a shop two doors away, and in 1902 to the double fronted shop opposite Trinity Methodist Church now the ladies hairdressers. In 1902 Mr James Snape passed away and Mr W Snape took charge, assisted by his brother Edward.

The Wolverhampton premises were opened in 1915 but the Wednesfield shop was kept on for some years after this, whilst Mr Snape continued to reside in Bolton Road. The house was later to be the home of Wednesfield Social Club. All the Snape family figured largely in local social life; both church and chapel, tennis and cricket clubs. Mr W Snape; being an ardent cricketer in his earlier days, whilst for over ten years he was a very active member of Wednesfield U.D.C. The growth and success of this business was like others of Wednesfield origin. Beginning in a small way, working hard personally for long hours with plenty of pluck and initiative.

Rising pressure of business in Wolverhampton led to Snape's leaving Wednesfield; their going regretted by many but they were still interested in its welfare, especially Mr W Snape, who was very active in spite of his 78 years, he often looked up old friends. Snape's went as a private limited company; the directors were Mr W Snape, Mr Peter Snape, his son and Mr Ted Snape his brother, the latter well remembered as a very droll comedian in local comic operettas years ago.

A celebrity Patron

Norman Wisdom of stage and screen fame when first appearing at Wolverhampton Grand Theatre several years ago, was fitted by Snape's for clothes and in spite of his rise to fame, they have been his tailors ever since, in fact they went to his Barnet (Herts) home to make further fittings.

1956

Wednesfield Laundry Ltd, Cross Street (24 hours bag wash service) You get a bag from us or our agents (deposit 3/-) and we wash the contents (Boiling wash only) up to 18lbs. Dry weight for 3/6 any day Monday to Friday, returned to you beautifully washed and ready for ironing in 24 hours. Did you ever use the bag wash service? Cross Street on the Hickman Estate would have been used by lots of people on that estate. Times have changed now and you can use the launderettes if you are desperate but things have moved on and most people now have washing machines; even my missus has one. As for hanging out the washing and ironing; well I claim that I have not got a clue how to do it. Kath accepts that I am useless at doing any washing or ironing. I can switch the washer on but that's about it. She has tried to teach me how to do it but I am a slow learner particularly with this sort of thing. After all, most blokes can switch the washing machine on but after that they are lost. Leave it to the women; they know more about that sort of thing than us blokes.

1957

Born at Wood End 1866

Mr S Dodd was born on the 22nd March 1866 and he was 91 in March of 1957. It was thought at the time that John Bull was the oldest trap maker living, but Mr Dodd could beat him by a few years. He then came to Wednesfield and started to work in the trap trade in 1878 for 3 shillings per week at Roberts (when John did and J Marshall) and finished up at Glover Bros when he was nearly 80. That must have been a record. Mr Dodd stayed with his daughter here and his other daughter lived in Canada. A Mr C Terry of Woden Way was his brother-in-law, formerly of North Street.

Ray Sambrook

Ray Sambrook made the headline of the sporting page of a national newspaper. He was expected to sign for Birmingham City for a five figure fee. But in the following weeks Birmingham considered Coventry's figure of £12.000 too high and lost interest in Ray, but it was felt that his club's decision to play him at centre-forward in a needle local derby, probably cost Ray his chance of playing in higher circles before the end of the season, for with only one more chance to watch him before the transfer deadline. Clubs were not to see him at his best in strange position for him, and in what is probably football's most difficult position.

Nevertheless, Ray played out the deadline with a good report in Coventry's 3-0 win over Swindon 'but it was Ray Sambrook whose ability caught the eye'. Who did Ray sign for? Do you know?

1957

Canal Rescue- Local Man's Timely Action

Quietly reading a book in Wednesfield Library, George James of Wolverhampton Road, Wednesfield was hastily summoned out late one afternoon to rescue a man who had fallen into the nearby canal. Just pausing to throw off his coat, George completed the rescue receiving assistance at the bank to get the man out of the water. A trainee draughtsman, he played cricket for his firm and centre-half for Wednesfield Youth Club soccer team.

He was also a member of Trinity Youth Club, well done George.

Herbert Harris 1957

Many residents in Wednesfield knew Herbert Harris better as the man with his bike, pushing it along the streets looking for fag ends or anything which he thought would be of some use to him. He resided in a hut made of old sheet iron and any old piece of tin at Backhouse End Lane (this lane was near Rookery Bridge). He lived his quiet life that way for many years, and although a vagrant he would very seldom speak to anyone but poor Herbert was not to be seen pushing his bike again; for on December 12th 1956 his body was recovered from the canal. Verdict: death from misadventure.

Social Take 'Johnson Cup'

Presentation night at the Social Club rounded off the most exciting season in the history of the Wednesfield Darts League, for it was not until the last 30 minutes that the issue was finally decided.

Three teams went into the last match with a chance of winning the league. Two were to play each other and at no game could the tension have been greater than in the struggle between the 'Star' and the 'Social'.

If the Star could win they had to await the result of the Wood End tussle between last year's winners, Castle 'A' and the previous year's winners 'Noah's Ark'. If the Social could win by a good margin of legs the league would be theirs on aggregate. There is little love lost between Noah's Ark and Castle and this gave the Social extra confidence. The social won well enough and left the Castle runners up with the Star in third and the New Inn in fourth place. A full season of see-saw struggle at the top but no talent money for Cinderella Conservative Club, one time leaders. Perhaps they could sustain their effort a little longer next season, when no doubt Noah's Ark would be back in the fight.

Before presenting the cup to the Social Club Councillor Arthur Jackson replied to the Chairman's observation that the Social's name completed the plinth and perhaps another cup for the competition. He congratulated Chairman Les Hughes and Secretary Aubrey Baugh on another great show in running the league and their fine effort for local charities. Some new names crept into the list of individual prizes and after being favourite to win the league average, Bert Jones (Social) lost his third and was caught by Dennis Millard (New Inn) to share first prize. Another social player Fred Cooper was to share first prize and for least darts (11) with George Careless of the Noah's Ark. Dennis Griffiths of Windsor made the highest start of 142 with Fred Peplow of the Castle Homing Society making the highest finish of 140.

Host of the New Crown Len Painter had to show his team how it should be done by making the highest score of 162 in the individual knockout, Vic Ricketts and Horace Banks of the Castle, beat George Turner and George Nicholls of the Star. Boys of the old brigade Jack Breakwell (Star and Bill Morris (Castle B) in their sixties, performed with credit, Jack having a great run in the knockout competition. George Brice (Pheasant) getting towards eighty, showed that he could still be reckoned with. A good variety show rounded off the evening but perhaps a more pleasing little ceremony to some of the darts players was the hand shake of Fred Cooper and Fred Snape, closing a feud brought about by a misunderstanding. The poser for the next season was, will they join the same team? Peacemaker George Nicholls had the answer; did they join the same team? Do you know?

Fig.39. Cllr Arthur Johnson presenting the thirteenth Johnson Cup to Aubrey Baker of the Social Club, league winners. Looking on left is hard working Secretary Aubrey Bough; and right, Chairman Les Hughes.

Gwynn Morgan Hall opened- Not a burden on general ratepayer

March 1957 saw the opening of Wednesfield's first civic building for communal and social purposes for council tenants. The building, named the Gwynn Morgan Hall in honour of the late clerk of the council was opened by Mr Clarence Haden, a member of the council for eleven years, and himself a close personal friend of Mr W G Morgan. The building was unique in the Midlands it was listed as a tenants meeting room under the Housing Acts of 1936-1952, being paid for from the housing revenue account and was thus not a burden upon the general ratepayer. The building cost about £5.000 to erect and weekly maintenance costs averaged £7.00 per week. Although the building was unique and Wednesfiled Urban District Council were to be congratulated on their enterprising lead, the opening ceremony only attracted 45 people of whom only eight were known to be council tenants. This, despite the fact that the ceremony took place on a mid-week evening to attract more people.

Fig.40. Opening ceremony. Mr A Pickering for the contractors, hands over the keys to Mr C Haden prior to the opening of the Gwynn Morgan Hall. Looking on are Mr T A Peacock, Cllr C T Squire and Cllr W Bargery.

A fine symbol

The building constructed by a local firm was to serve residents on the Moathouse, Lichfield Road and Perry Hall estates, a population of about 4,300. It consisted of a main assembly room with a ten foot deep stage, Kitchenette and cloakrooms. Heating was by electric tubular heaters, thermostatically controlled. A management committee of ten were responsible for running the centre. Six of which were councillors and four tenants. They operated for a trial period of three months. A condition of using the building, which was open for social gatherings and receptions, was that no alcoholic drinks can be bought, sold or consumed on the premises. In declaring the centre open, Mr Haden said that all using the hall had a fine symbol to follow in the life of Gwynn Morgan. "He was a kindly Christian man who made his mark in this district during four brief years". This was a tribute amongst equals, for Mr Haden was one who made an immense contribution to the rising development of Wednesfield. Mr Haden warmly welcomed new residents to the district through the overspill scheme. "They would find Wednesfield a friendly place in which to live" he said. He was also glad to see the urban list of priorities continually being tackled in the order of previous councils, namely, houses first, roads and transport next, then shopping facilities and finally community centres.

"All residents have proof that the council was doing its job and wants overspill people to belong to Wednesfield," ended Mr Haden. Did you use the Gwynn Morgan Hall? I think that I went there for a reception in the seventies but I can't remember that much of what the place was like. Do you remember Clarence Haden? Well I used to be friends with his son Freddy; if my memory serves me well they lived in Amos Lane and I believe that their garden used to back onto the gardens of Tithe Road, somewhere by Oakleys and Aultons, if that sounds right or could it be Horton's? I will get shot if I have not got that right because I used to knock about with Johnny Horton. With the Gwynn Morgan Hall I believe that they ran into financial difficulties after about two to three years after opening, "don't we all?" but they all sorted things out and it continued as a venue for the overspill locals. Are you an overspill local?

Diamond Wedding Celebrations- August 15th 1957

Mr and Mrs Joseph Onions, 101 Lichfield Road, Wednesfield marked the celebration of their diamond wedding by holding a dinner at the Prestwood Arms Hotel, where 61 guests headed by their two sons, John Henry and Frank came to do them honour. A delightful musical programme was rendered by May Hough (soprano) and William

Turner (baritone) whilst Zena Cooper was a brilliant pianist. Amongst numerous telegrams of congratulations received was one from Buckingham Palace from her Majesty the Queen. Mr and Mrs Onions were very proud indeed of this. Mr and Mrs Onions grew old gracefully and retained their sense of humour; indeed Mr Onions who was 86 and who had lived some 73 years of his long life in Wednesfield, was addicted to 'having the gloves on' with Mrs Onions (just his fun of course) but it always ends in a draw he said, so that they could start afresh the next morning. Mrs Onions was 81; they lived most of their 60 years of married life in Lichfield Road, chiefly in the same house. Well done to Mr and Mrs Onions for 60 years of married life and for receiving a telegram from the Queen.

Golden Wedding Anniversary

Married on September 4th 1907 in Alstonfield Methodist Church, Derbyshire; Mr and Mrs Phillip Condlyffe of 57 Victoria Road celebrated their golden wedding anniversary on September 4th 1957. Mr Condlyffe was a member of the Staffordshire Constabulary until his retirement upon 28 years of service and he was stationed at Moseley Village, Willenhall. The Condlyffe's had been resident in Wednesfield since 1928 and had grown very attached to the district. Their daughter Mrs Elsie Bridgewood lived next door to them with her husband Alec and their daughter Janet. Across the street at number 46 lived their son Mr John Condlyffe with his wife May and their daughter Jennifer. As a policeman on the beat Mr Condlyffe had some stirring memories of years ago when policemen had to proceed in pairs when on duty at weekends. In those days public houses were open all day and its frequently happened that a man might spend all his weeks wages in a day's drinking in the pub, 'just like today' I can hear you say. Mr Condlyffe had witnessed many scenes of poverty and heartbreak caused through drink but he asserts that today much less open drinking goes on. The brews drunk are also less potent he said and the drunken man, once a common sight is now rarely seen in our streets. The Condlyffe's have long been lifelong Methodists and much of their life was centered on Trinity Church, Wednesfield where they were members and Mr Condlyffe was a leader and trustee of

Trinity Church. We wish them well and congratulate them on fifty years of married life.

Wednesfield Methodism 1957

Some of us are thankful that the gospel of our gracious and hallowed redeemer offers a second chance to the morally fatigued and the spiritually depressed. We are grateful that the divine goodwill seeks us out and offers to make all things new. The slate of our misdemeanours, our tawdry sins and cheap rebellion wiped clean and we can start afresh. Praise God! He holds nothing against us. Thus the Church following the supreme dispensation of the Holy Spirit gives that second chance to those who fall or fail. There is perennial hope of a good recovery; the gospel is the story of new beginnings; the Church is the home of the morally lapsed and the spiritually defaulting. The commencement of another connexional year is a time of new beginnings; a fresh start, a second chance is offered. The Church caters for those who have not made the grade, who have tried but not succeeded. In Christ 'old things are done away, all things become new'. To those tired and listless, jaded and worn out in their quest for a victorious life, the Church opens wide its doors in fellowship and love. Everyone may come in. No one knocking is denied admission, only the self-righteous, the hypocritical and the religious prig enter not, for they exclude themselves. Into this saving ministry all are welcome; you are included. The beginning of another Methodist year is a time of new beginnings. May it mark a spiritual epoch in your life when you, dear reader begin afresh!

Fig.41. This picture is prior to 1957. Barclays Bank had not yet been built. Frost's the chemist is on the right of the picture with the Rose and Crown next door.

1959- Homing

At the annual dinner and prize presentation of the Wednesfield Homing Society, Chairman of the Council Councillor SJ Perks had to learn of another sport that had got 'hold of' quite a number of the districts sporting fraternity and in order to further the Chairmans education in this sphere which could boast such distinguished persons as the late King George who maintained lofts at Sandringham and Sir Gordon Richards, one of the wonders of nature is the homing instincts of the pigeon. To expect any success a fancier must start with birds of a good strain for breeding purposes, otherwise an already expensive sport would become more costly. Training starts when the bird is approximately six weeks old and is acquainted with the surroundings of its own loft. The birds are put into a 'training basket' and taken about one mile from their loft and released to make their own way home. When they have learned the 'first mile' they are taken greater distances in as near as possible a straight line along the route over which they are to be raced.

When the homing instinct is fully developed the next phase (one of the most important) is commenced. This is trapping and is important for having flown well for 200 miles; a bird could lose a race by the time taken to settle into its loft.

British railways help extensively in the training and racing of homing pigeons. First the birds are sent on a small journey generally to Kidderminster and relaxed. Then as training proceeds, greater journeys are undertaken with the town of Bath being preferred by most local fanciers. Here the birds are again released and start on their long flight back to their own lofts.

Races are mainly from the English South Coast and 'across the water' from French and Spanish sea ports before being dispatched to the race point, birds are taken to club headquarters where a stamped rubber ring is placed around one leg. The birds travel in race panniers which are accompanied by the club's conveyer who attends to watering and feeding en route. Then comes the time to see how successful the training has been for the late Saturday afternoon sees the fancier patiently scanning the skies suddenly alerted as his bird comes in sight. With bated breath he removes the ring and rushes off

to the Castle Inn, Wood End only to find that Chris Cole has been there already.
Popular Chris Cole the year's average winner had been successful over the past few years and his name regularly appeared in the 'Express & Star' homing returns when he and other 'Castle' members were with the Wolverhampton Central Club.
Councillor A Johnson paid tribute to Mr and Mrs Hargrave for the great help they had been in the formation and success of the club and hoped that if the Brewery did not rebuild the 'Castle' they would at least enlarge the present premises in order to give these good people the facilities to cater at 'home' for such enjoyable evenings as this.
Secretary Jim Hadley was deservedly congratulated on the expert way that he handled the 71 strong membership of the club. The success of the evening was largely due to Jim and to the accomplished chairmanship of Mr Tom Hickman.
Together with the Chairman of the Council and Mrs Perks and Vice Chairman Councillor A Johnson were two other distinguished visitors, the husband and wife team of officials of the federation Mr and Mrs B Brown, President and Secretary respectively.

Fig.42. Castle Inn 1955. Is that Jimmy Lampoils next door? Notice the wall that surrounded Wood End School.

Town Topics November 1959

It was announced that the Tettenhall Magistrates Court (which covered the urban district of Wednesfield) would be making arrangements in the New Year to hold a Domestic Court bi-monthly, to deal with Wednesfield cases in a court room at the Council Offices, Alfred Squire Road. This was indeed a step in the right direction, along with the setting up of an interviewing office for the probation work in this district.

The council looked forward with hope to the possibility of an official Magistrated Court for Wednesfield, in view of the rapid and continuing development of our town.

The traffic hold ups which occur daily in the High Street were certainly growing in intensity, but the tragedy was that this state of affairs could not possibly be altered for two or three years unless the redevelopment of the High Street shopping centre could be bought forward at a very different rate than had been evident during the previous few years.

A complete ban of parking either sides of the High Street was the only alleviation that could be suggested but that did not appeal to the shopping fraternity, either buyers or sellers and so the problem remained.

Fig.43. More traffic jams in the High Street late 1950's.

Fig.44. Traffic congestion in the High Street late 50's.

Fig.45. Again, traffic jams in the High Street.

The newly acquired Depot of the Urban District Council at Wood End was now being used, but despite its cost and size the council had not thought fit to indicate in a suitable manner at the entrance gates what it was.

Fig.46. Gates to the Council Yard, Moathouse Lane. The sign on the tree says it all.

Fig.47. Moathouse Lane dump.

Fig.48. The new Post Office being built at the rear of the old one.

Fig.49. The new Post Office and flats opened 21st October 1959; one flat being hairdressers; Dorothy Gelthorp and Ann Palmer.

Wednesfield's Garden of Remembrance opened

The Garden of Remembrance was officially opened on Sunday November 8th 1959. After the usual Armistice Day Service in the Parish Church on Sunday November 8th, held in the afternoon, the Clergy, Congregation and members of the council moved across the way for the official opening of the Garden of Remembrance.

The Chairman of the Council, Councillor A Johnson expressed the hope that residents would respect this ground and at the same time enjoy the pleasant layout which he stated would be cared for by the Local Authority.

Councillors Wootton and Bargery supported the Chairman in these sentiments. The Dedication Ceremony was performed by the Vicar, the Rev F Norman Lewis, assisted by the Rev F LeNoury, Methodist Minister.

Fig.50. Garden of Remembrance 2011.

One does, feel on looking at the Garden, a local point of suitable design would make it possible to hold a yearly remembrance service like so many of our towns and villages throughout the country, just previous to the morning service in our various churches so that at the appropriate time of 11:00am we could stand in unison with our

countrymen throughout the land and join in the national tribute. With goodwill and cooperation this could be a reality for next Armistice Sunday.
Yes that was great, a real good thing to do and the folk of Wednesfield really took to Armistice Sunday just the same as everyone around the country, and it's called respect for those that laid down their lives in the two World Wars. Yet here we are in Wednesfield's Garden of Remembrance in May 2011 where some low life has stolen the plates that depict the names of those wonderful, brave soldiers that gave their lives so that we could be here in a free Great Britain, just what would they get for those plates? Not a lot, they probably realised when they stole them that they would be hard to get shut of. I would not be surprised if they weren't at the bottom of the canal. Let's get those plates returned as soon as possible.

Memories of Wednesfield

When I was young things were quite different than what they are today.
My memories of Wednesfield are that we had hard times but you had to forget difficult times and remember more the good times; of which there were plenty. Everyone has their own personal memories of growing up in Wednesfield. Mine, like most folk start when you went to school, how you made friends, and how you performed in various subjects like; History, Maths and Sport. There were only three where I was concerned; if I had to add another subject then it would be Music.
Sport was a great leveller of a person because that's where you could show your true self but in Football or Rugby you had the chance to show what you could do. I suppose that my best sports were football and cross country running. Yes I was good at those two but so were a lot of other kids. I can say with confidence that there were a lot of good footballers in Wednesfield in the 1960's, a lot of us could have made it but we didn't. For no matter how good you were, you had to be in the right place at the right time to be noticed. You only need to talk to some of the lads from the 60's and they all agree that there were a lot of good footballers in Wednesfield but very few got

anywhere. What about the girls? What sports could they get noticed at? This is not my subject but it could have been the same for them in whatever sport they were good at; Hockey, Netball and Running I should imagine would be their sports where they could really excel at. But whatever sport we were good at, we enjoyed all the sports that we had at our schools. Most of us loved every minute at school although you are not aware of it at the time. It's only when you look back that you realise; yes they were happy times and back then you could not wait to leave to start work. You take on commitments and you get on that treadmill. You go to work to pay the bills for whatever you do, it's always to earn money to pay for this and that and that's the way things are generation after generation. Play the Carpenters record its 'Yesterday Once More' it might just make you think of times gone by.

Yes when someone asks you for your memories of Wednesfield you will probably refer to your school days in Wednesfield. For that's where our lives really started; school days.

Fig.51. Thompsons paper shop on the left, Regal Cinema, The Wesleyan Church, The Royal Oak and of course the 59 bus.

22. 1960's

Springhill drapers opened 1961 Ltd
Nursery Furniture and Prams etc... Pedigree Vantage Pram choice of duo-tone colour schemes, cash price £18.15.6, no deposit, 39 weekly payments of 11/2.
Wearwell Pushchair folds in one easy action, foot brake £3.3.0
Pedigree Toddle Chair, lightwood chair with gay transfer and play beads £2.10.0.
Pedigree Dropside Cot size 47 in x 24in, half bow ends. Furnished cellulose and attractive transfers. £7.8.6 matress to match- £2.19.6
Pedigree Cosy Crib new colours and designs, folds flat when not in use £4.4.0
Pedigree Pram Mattress soft and hygienic 17/6, pillow to match 11/3.
Hey it would be great if you could buy today at those prices. Can you remember Springhill Drapers of 39/41 Lichfield Road next to the cross Guns? Springhill Drapers opened in 1961; this later became the Penguin Freezer Shop. Can you remember this and did you buy any frozen items from there?

Fig.52. Lichfield Road corner of Taylor Street about 1960/61. Building being built was Springhill Drapers, it opened in Spring 1961.

Fig.53. Duke Street 30-11-77. The Vine is on the left, at the time it was Courage Beers. Springhill Drapers can be seen in the background.

Lewis Garages Ltd

Evening and weekend servicing. Look at these prices:
A short service 10/- (plus oils)
A medium service 12/6 (plus oils)
And if you have time to spare, stay and make a thorough inspection of your car while the job is being done.

Lewis Garages Ltd, Lichfield Road, Wednesfield
Corner of Linthouse Lane. Telephone: Wolverhampton 32197
Paravan Pet Supplies
Everything you need for your pets. Guinea pigs / foreign birds / Tortoises / Goldfish / Fresh dogmeat daily from local slaughterhouse. Poodle trimming / three mast pigeon corn.
High Street, Wednesfield (opposite the Church) Telephone: Wolverhampton 32017

Squires Hardware Limited

Squires Hardware Limited, Ironmongers – builder's merchants Save yourself time and money by getting gardening tools of quality! We also feature garden rollers, mowers and wheelbarrows by all the leading makers. Garden list available on request. The Rookery, Wednesfield Tel 32671.

Fig.54. Bits and pieces Rookery Street, corner of Hall Street; formerly Squires Hardware shop 21-1-1976.

Fig.55. Rookery Street looking towards the four shops, now in the Black Country Museum. Car sales on site of Squires Hardware shop.

Fig.56. Rear of Rookery Street 1930's. Proper old houses of Wednesfield.

1962

Wednesfield welcomes the Queen 24th May

Cheering crowds line streets on Towns great day. A gaily decorated Alfred Squire Road, including a wonderful display of flowers in front of the Council Offices welcomed the Queen on her short walk in Wednesfield during her journey from Wolverhampton to Walsall. Her Majesty, smiling in the sunshine and wearing a beige coat with hat to match stepped out of the Royal car onto the carpet and walked to the red canopy erected in front of the entrance to the Council Offices. There she was met by a number of Councillors, amongst who were the new Chairman of the Council H.P Fitzmaurice and his wife. When the Queen stepped forward to sign the visitor's books for Wednesfield and Willenhall, she picked up the pen and remarked "Will it write?" The Queen signed the books and was then handed a composure and presented with pink roses and white lilies by petite Carol Burns aged seven of 29 Pickering Road.

Fig.57. Miss Carol Ann Burns of Neachells Lane County Primary School presents a bouquet of miniature pink roses to Her Majesty.

The Queen spent a little time talking to Councillors and members of the public, before she made her way in the Royal Car down Lichfield Road where she was welcomed by tremendous cheering from 6,000 schoolchildren waving to the Queen as she went by. We all had small flags to wave and it seemed like we stood for hours before we caught a glimpse of her passing by. Come to think of it, it was a couple of hours-still it was worth it.

Prior to the Queen coming to Wednesfield, a ballot was held at all Wednesfield Primary Schools to decide upon the girl who would present the Queen with a bouquet on her visit.

Fig.58. Her Majesty tells the Chairman of the council H.P Fitzmaurice how much she enjoyed the visit.

The eventual winner was Linda Helena Wytha. Another name drawn was Carol Burns, the reserve. Something must have happened for Carol presented the flowers to the Queen. Perhaps Linda was unwell? The Queen's visit on 24th May 1962 is one of the most special days in the annuals of Wednesfield, it must have been a great day for Carol also. Well apart from waving at the Queen in the crowd way back then I actually got a bit closer in June 1994 when she officially opened Wolverhampton Racecourse. I worked at the Racecourse then and she walked past me, I was three feet from her, the racecourse opened on Boxing Day 1993 but as stated it was officially opened in the June of 1994, was you in the crowd at Wednesfield in 1962?

1963

Mothers should not be forced to work says MP September 1963

It is quite wrong for mothers to be forced to go to work in order to obtain a standard of living which is theirs by right says Miss Jennie Lee, Labour MP for the Cannock constituency.

Miss Lee accompanied by Wednesfield Labour Councillors was addressing shoppers in Wednesfield Market Place on Saturday during a visit to the Town. After touring the market place Miss Lee addressed shoppers from a loudspeaker van and told them that she had been collecting evidence to test the claim that a family of four could feed quite well on £5 a week. "I do not profess to be a very good housewife, but I do find this statement hard to believe" she said. She spoke of a widowed pensioner who said she could spend £3 a week on food "with the greatest of ease" and of one family she met who spent £10 a week on food without luxuries. An analysis of national incomes showed that there was less than £5 a week going into more than 4,000,000 homes in this country and less than £10 a week going into about 10,000,000 homes. "I would like to see everyone earning a decent family wage so that a comfortable standard of living can be maintained without the mother going out to work if she does not wish to do so. What is quite wrong is that mothers are forced out to work to get a standard of life which nowadays, is perfectly proper to have she said. She was looking forward to the next labour government which would be profoundly concerned with the everyday problems of the home including the food bill. "We want the kind of Britain where everyone is given the chance of a job with fair wages and fair conditions," declared Miss Lee. "We have a long way to go yet before we can say we have reached that position".

Fig.59. Karen Billingsley aged four months with her parents Mr a Mrs Richard Billingsley of 18 Lich Avenue, caught the eye of Miss Jennie Lee MP, and Labour councillors in Wednesfield Market Place.

Some advertisements for Wednesfield

In September 1963 adverts in local papers were as follows:
J Kenyon & Son
Austin Morris and Ford Reatail Dealers
New Austin Morris and Fords for early delivery.
New Ford Cortina Estate car, Aqua Blue and White, £683-5-5
New Austin 1100 Deluxe with heater, Tartan Red £623-0-0
New Morris Mini Super Deluxe Saloons Choice of colour £419-19-2
New Morris Mini Van Deluxe with Heater Fawn £387-0-0
A selection of our used cars:
1962 Austin A/60 Deluxe as new maroon with white flash, 9000 miles only £665
1960 Austin A/40 Farina Deluxe very low mileage £370
1959 Jaguar overdrive, disc brakes, one owner £545
1959 Sunbeam Rapier Convertible £450
1959 Ford Anglia Deluxe, two-tone grey £345
1958 Ford Consul Deluxe, radio etc... £340
1958 Hillman Minx Deluxe, very good £305
1958 Ford Anglia Deluxe Saloon, very clean £225
1956 Ford Popular, black, many extras, heater £99
1959 Vespa G.S Scooter £70
All vehicles MOT tested where required, Wednesfield Garage, Wolverhampton Road, Wednesfield. Ring: Wolverhampton 31372 and 32407. That's a great advert, just look at the prices. How cheap are those? A 1959 Jaguar for £545, it's a shame I can't afford it or I would give Kenyons a call. The 1956 Ford Popular at £99 is about what I can afford, if you could buy those cars today at those prices, well you don't need me to tell you that you would be able to make a small fortune, never mind, there's always the lottery.

1965- August 1965

August 1965 saw work start on the new £30.000 Church of St Gregory in Blackhalve Lane, Wednesfield which was to replace the previous dual purpose building.
The completion of the new Church would mark the end of an 11 year crusade to establish St Gregory's as a Parish Church.

The building was expected to be completed by the beginning of August 1966 and would be twice the size of the previous Church hall. It would seat a congregation of about 400 in contemporary surroundings.

The priest in charge of St Gregory's, the Rev E Downing and the parishioners had been working constantly to raise money for the building. Even the Sunday school children keen to take part in the fund raising effort, contributed the money for a new bell. Other Churches too had helped.

The Organ, to be installed was originally in Heath Town Congregational Church, now demolished.

The new Church will rise on land adjacent to the present building, which is to become the Parish Hall. Because of its dual purpose properties this could never have become a Parish Church as it was not used solely for divine worship.

On September 4th the ground on the site of the new Church was symbolically broken during an open air service, to mark the commencement of building.

23. Bentley Canal opened in 1843.

Fig.60. Bentley Canal; is that the tube works in the background?

Fig.61. Bentley Canal near to Neachells Lane; once a hive of activity and was largely abandoned in the early 1960's.

Fig.62. Bentley Canal; now the site of Bentley Bridge Shopping Centre.

Fig.63. The Tube Works, top left is Yale & Towne. To the right of the 's' bend prior to the Yale stood 'Shed Farm'. Bentley Canal is visible running alongside the Tube.

24. Temperance Hall, Hall Street

By the time you read this, things will have moved on a bit from 24th May 2011, for that's the day that I opposed Sainsbury's proposals to demolish the Old Temperance Hall to make way for an extension of their car park to create another 74 parking spaces.

This is what I put forward on behalf of the folk of Wednesfield at the planning meeting held at the Civic Centre Planning Applications:

Every time a new development is heard about, shivers run down the spine of every local historian who collectively fear that soon there will be so much of the Black Country swept away the place will be hardly recognisable. A prime example of this situation has just come to light in Wednesfield with the proposal by Sainsbury's to demolish the old Temperance Hall that dates back to the early 1860's, first used by the Salvation Army and then used as a theatre and cinema named the Tivoli-smack.

Fig.64. The Old Temperance Hall. Photo explains it all.

Fig.65. The old windows still visible in brickwork.

Fig.66. June / July 2011 front view.

Fig.67. The Old Temperance Hal 1960's then used as a body repair shop (cars) not humans.

It is now 50 years ago this year that Wednesfield Urban District Council made the decision to demolish the Regal Cinema in the name of progress to build a supermarket there. The decision back then angered the folk of Wednesfield. The folk of Wednesfield need the Old Temperance Hall to remain so that our kids and their kids have something left so that they can get a feel of how things were back in those good old days in Wednesfield.

Fig.68. Tivoli Theatre Hall Street incorporated into Hill Brothers builder's yard.

We need to retain what heritage we can because most of it has already been lost, let's not make the same mistakes over and over again.

Let's not forget that Wednesfield holds a prominent place in history with the famous battle between the Anglo Saxons and the Vikings taking place here on 5/6th August 910AD.

Because we want to keep this building intact we feel that a compromise could be reached between the folk of Wednesfield and Sainsbury's. I would like to read you the petition that we have which is self-explanatory; written by a prominent Wednesfield person.

'We, the people of Wednesfield call upon Sainsbury's and Wolverhampton City Council to include the former Tempetrance Hall in Wednesfield in their new developments retaining the history and heritage of Wednesfield and call upon them to drop their proposals to demolish this heritage building. Wednesfield as a community has suffered more than most Black Country towns from the loss of its ancient heritage, delivering an innovative planning proposal which incorporates a use for the building, would be applauded in the same way that Sainsbury's delivered a store using the former St George's Church in Wolverhampton. The building is a heritage asset and it is being proposed to demolish this for a car park! I appeal to you on behalf of the folk of Wednesfield to refuse the proposal to demolish a building that is part of Wednesfield's heritage.

That's what was put forward to the planning committee, not forgetting that you had only four minutes to make your point. That's all the time you are allowed, no wonder these big companies get there proposals pushed through. Well let's look at some buildings or heritage sites that Wednesfield has lost over the years.

The Bentley Canal to make way for, well what a coincidence; Bentley Bridge shopping centre. The canal was built in the 1800s but that did not matter, it was filled in and redeveloped.

What about Alcocks Farm by New Cross, demolished. What is it now? A car park.

The Regal Cinema demolished In March of 1962, what for? A supermarket. What a total waste.

The Ideal Cinema or Smack in Rookery Street, burned down by arsonists in November 1990. The shops in Rookery Street that ran from the Royal Oak to Squires Hardware corner of Hall Street, these shops now in the Black Country Museum. The old Police Station just over Rookery Bridge on the right, demolished early 70s. Those terraced houses in Well Lane and the café all gone.

Remember those six or so houses that ran up to the canal from the shop opposite the Dog & Partridge (Trubshaws) gone. Nothing has replaced them. The terraced houses that made up Hadleys Fold along from the Dog & Partridge in Neachells Lane gone. What's there now? A car park.

The Civil Defence on Regal Fields, what's there now? Well you could say the Police Station although the Civil Defence club was behind that a bit, well I suppose that's some sort of defence so we'll let that go.

The old Church School, what's there now? No comment.

Hickman Estate, no comment.

Church in the cemetery, the Old St Thomas' Mortuary Church, gone. Nothing there now.

There are more but I will not go on and on, all I will say is that a lot of them were unnecessary but what I will say is this. What is safe in Wednesfield? Not a lot, not from this committee from the planning department from Wolverhampton because they will approve any plans by any big business if they say it means jobs. These jobs being put forward by Sainsbury's, 80 what jobs are they? Saturday part time jobs and Sunday's. Who is there to keep check on the number of jobs actually created?
I did write to HRH Prince Charles, perhaps by the end of the year he might get in touch with me. I put my phone number in the letter; he could call and reverse the charges. Hold on a minute, don't do that Charles my phone bill is sky high. Plug.
So here we are, not that much left in Wednesfield now from the good old days. Let's have a rough look around to see what the City Council have left us for the time being.
Well, we have St Thomas' Church, they wouldn't dare but I wouldn't put it past them.
The Dog & Partridge one of the oldest buildings left here in Wednesfield; no that will stay. What about the Pyle Cock? Well that's in the Rookery so that will have to be careful; prime site for a car park.
What about those places that have recently closed like the Old Drill Hall, Edward the Elder School, TocH, Graiseley Lane or even the old library what's waiting for these? What about the café next to Barclays? No it's ok there, so where else do you see that Wolverhampton planning department will allow to be redeveloped? Anywhere except a pub. Having said all this I am no stick in the mud, I believe in change and we have to move forward but in moving forward let's still retain some of our past.
With the way that Bentley Bridge is going, what with the extension of Sainsbury's and ASDA Living coming here. To me it means that the traders in the High Street are going to suffer, the market is struggling so what are they going to do with all the expansion of Bentley Bridge going on? We have already lost one butcher and a couple of shops are now empty. Is this a sign of the future? Very few shops in the High Street, most of the trade done on Bentley Bridge.

Any predictions from you folk of Wednesfield on what heritage we are to lose next at the hands of the City of Wolverhampton Planning Committee? Answers on a postcard please.
It has just come to light about arsonists setting fire to the former Larry's Industrial Tyre building in on Wolverhampton Road, Wednesfield on Tuesday evening at 8.00pm 31st May.

Fig.69. Part of the building that's left after the fire, once part of Alcocks Farm.

The Express & Star reported this incident the following evening saying 'squatter hurt in blaze'. A man believed to have been squatting in the building was taken to nearby New Cross Hospital with smoke inhalation. The road was cordoned off today while structural engineers assessed the damage. Large sections of the garage's tiled roof were destroyed by the flames. Today, group commander Ben Diamond said "The elderly gentleman inside was taken to hospital by paramedics." Let's not forget that these buildings were at one time part of Alcocks Farm, and that has been demolished. The question is,

are the buildings going to be demolished? Answer is yes they have now been demolished.
Since writing this piece I have now had a response from Clarence House. Read as follows:

From the Office of TRH
The Prince of Wales and The Duchess of Cornwall.
29th June 2011

Dear Mr Fellows
Thank you for your letter of 22nd May to The Prince of Wales in connection with a proposal by Wolverhampton City Council to develop the site currently occupied by the Temperance Hall in Wednesfield.
His Royal Highness is most grateful to you for taking the trouble to bring this particular case and your concerns to his attention. However, I regret The Prince Of Wales position makes it difficult for him to become personally involved with planning decisions of this nature. Nevertheless your letter has been reviewed and we would suggest that you might find it helpful to refer to the following organisation that may be able to help:
SAVE Britain's Heritage
70 Cowcross Street
London
ECIM 6EJ
Tel: 020 7253 3500

I am so sorry to send you such a disappointing reply, but trust that you understand. Thank you once again for writing to His Royal Highness, who has asked me to send you his very best wishes.
Yours Sincerely

I have to say that it's wonderful to get a reply and yes it's obvious that His Royal Highness cannot get involved. I thank them for their advice and their best wishes, thank you. It's wonderful writing paper that the letter is written on and the envelope with ER stamped on it along with the BUCKINGHAM PALACE stamp mark. Thanks again.

25. Pubs that were trading in Wednesfield in the 1800's

The Cross Guns; a Joshua Hope kept it in 1850/60.
The Dog & Partridge was kept by Samuel Marston in 1834 and Edward Marston in the 1850s.
Angel; a Luke Nichols kept it in 1834 and Luke Marshall in the 1850s followed by a J Marshall in the 1860s.
Rose and Crown; Esther Taylor in 1834 and F Peace in the 1850s/60s.
The Crown was kept by a J Marshall in 1834.
The Old Tiger; Joseph Tomkys was there in 1834.
The Albion in 1860 was kept by a J Tonks.
New Inns; J Tomkys 1834 and the 1850s/60s.
Royal Oak 1850s; Mrs E Corkindale and a Mr H Corbett in the 1860s.
All these pubs were trading in the 1800s; it seems so long ago and yet.
In 1938 the license from the Whitehouse Inn near Olinthus Bridge was transferred to the Albion on Lichfield Road.

The Dog and Partridge

Well the Dog and Partridge dates back to over 400 years. We know that John Gregory was at the Dog in the 1890's up until 1915, that's when Mr Ernest Gregory with Miss Kate Gregory and another sister; Miss Florence Gregory who died in the early 1940's took over the Dog and Partridge which has been in the Gregory family since at least the 1880's.
Miss Kate Gregory was the youngest of the children; two of whom Mr Percy Gregory aged 76 were still alive in 1963. The Dog and Partridge was put up for sale in 1963 after Mr Ernest Gregory had died that year aged 85; four months later Miss Kate Gregory died, she was 73.
At the time Mr Percy Gregory said it was not yet known if the Inn would stay in the family. He recounted the great pride his sister took in looking after the historic Inn, until about 1953 it had its own brew of beer to offer. Sitting in the inglenook by a blazing fire, he told how his sister polished up the old horse brasses and brought up a black mirrored surface on the 120 year old coalbrookdale grate in the

'kitchen' where generations of Wednesfield people have sat. The Inn at the time was being run by Mr Percy Gregory, Junior.

In her younger days, Miss Gregory was a keen tennis player, and was for years a staunch member of the former Wednesfield Amateur Operatic Society. Wolverhampton and Dudley Breweries purchased the Inn for £37,000. A spokesman for the brewery at the time said "I think it is reasonable to say that at some time, The Dog and Partridge will be rebuilt, for the present it will continue as it is.

As the High Street improvement line–marked by the immediately adjoining new shops development, runs behind the existing Inn premises. A new Public House would be built further back on the site but it is not yet known when that will be. Well we all know that it never was demolished or rebuilt.

Another Wednesfield site with redevelopment possibilities was also on the market at that time, it was the former Ideal Cinema in Rookery Street, a price of £4,500 was being asked for the property.

Fig.70. Roof repairs to Dog & Partridge High Street about 1900.

Fig.71. After roof repairs. Mr & Mrs J Gregory in doorway

Fig.72. Early view of the High Street; no tram lines or cars; just a horse and cart.

26. Aerial View circa 1974

Dismantlers yard on the Orchard building site to the right of William Bentley flats. Orchard buildings ran up to Duke Street. With this photo you can see that the Church field gardens had not yet been built on between the gardens of Tithe Road and Taylor Street.

Fig.73. Aerial view circa 1974.

A few other things worth noting; the Dog and Partridge still has a bowling green, the market is still on the same site and the Royal Oak still stands.

33. Speakers Corner

The Royal Oak, 78 Rookery Street. Mrs Sybil Ansell.

The Royal Oak stood on the corner of Well Lane and Rookery Street. Mrs Sybil Ansell lived there from about 1929 until the war years 1940. The Royal Oak had four bedrooms and as you can see from the photograph the beer was Butlers, although at one time it was home brewed beer there.

Sybil says that there were some lovely etched windows in the big bar, showing King Charles hiding in the oak tree at Boscobel. I used to bring my school chums to find the King in that window. I wonder what happened to that. My father-in-law served in the Wednesfield Police during the war alongside Mr Tedstill who had a cycle shop up towards the Smack cinema. I had my first cycle from there in the 1940s. Thanks Sybil, those windows would be worth a small fortune today. Where are they?

Fig.74. Royal Oak, corner of Rookery Street.

Fig.75. Cricket team. My father Arthur Tonks first on the left, middle row. Third one is his brother Frank Tonks.

Joyce Bartlett

I left Wednesfield in 1939 (April) when I had just left school. My dad had got a job at Rolls Royce. They left in 1938; I stayed with my gran in Wood End Road to finish school.

I lived a few doors from Sylvia Parry in Woden Avenue, although we didn't go to the same school (We did go to Woden Avenue Juniors together). I went to Lichfield Road, we have remained friends for 71 years, we have always kept in touch and when she was in the Land Army I wrote to her which is a wonderful record of friendship. We have met occasionally, she kept me in touch with a boy I knew (and liked) at school and I married him in 1948. He came to work at Rolls Royce when he came out of the army. He was Ron Bartlet whose family lived all their lives at number 12 North Avenue, Nordley Hill. His sister died last year, Mrs Perrins, it's now so strange my cousins daughter now lives in the house. There was a big family of Bartletts, six boys, two girls, they are sadly all dead now, my husband died in 1988.

I have such happy memories of Wednesfield, we had a lovely childhood. My uncle kept the farm and outdoor pub in Wood End and my gran lived in a lovely detached old house that was knocked down to widen the road but there was enough land to build another house. My auntie lived in it and when she died her children sold it. How times change. I remember so well Hilda Anslows and Jimmy Lamp oils. My gran would send me for a penny gas mantle.

We came back to Wednesfield every holiday, even when my gran died we came to Aunties and of course to see my husband's family. A couple of years ago friends bought me here. I called at my sister-in-laws and saw my grans old house, but Wednesfield is much changed from the little village that I grew up in. I spent 14 very happy years there and to me it will always be home.

I think you have done so well to have written your book. My niece is always telling me that I should write things down but at 85 I'm afraid it's a bit late in the day.

So thank you for bringing back some happy memories of Wednesfield.
My best wishes and a happy new year to the folks of Wednesfield.
Joyce Bartlett now living in Crewe.

Joyce that was great and to be friends for 71 years, well that's fantastic. That's 71 Christmas's. Do you recall your first Christmas present?

Peter Massey

I was born in Woden Avenue in 1949 where I lived with my parents and two sisters Rosemary and Sylvia.

Rosemary now lives in Gillingham, Kent. Sylvia lives in Hull Yorkshire. At five years of age I went to Woden Avenue School where I first met Roy Simpson (shrimpy). I spent many happy hours playing in the Legion fields at the back of our house. The Cottage Homes were at the end of Woden Avenue, that's where children with no parents, or perhaps unwanted were taken to live in those homes.

The Cottage Homes were run by Mr and Mrs Macho, any children that were late back from school were caned, and they used to have to walk to school in all weathers to the Prestwood Road School in Heath Town.

Fig.76. Back row (L-R) Headmaster Mr Steephenson, Robert Boersma, Peter Massey, Tony Simcock, Keith Banks, John Robinson, Stephen Bonehill, Teacher Mr Owen. Front row: Michael Griffiths, Stephen Lewis, Roy Simpson, Peter Collins, Linden Lloyd.

At the age of eleven I moved from Woden Avenue School to St Thomas' Church of England School in 1961. That was for only one term until March End School was opened in January 1962.
I played football for the school team, oh what a team with the legendary 'Clippy' Banks in goal, his cousin Archie Richards played inside forward. The captain was 'Corkey' Bickley. Did March End School really have the best looking girls in Wednesfield?

WOLVERHAMPTON CHRONICLE—PAGE 21

SPORTS EXTRA

Here is the March End Secondary Modern Boys School football team which won the South-East Staffordshire Senior Schools Shield. The team is from left to right (back row): Kenneth Blower, Arthur Richards, Keith Banks, Walter Bickley, John Chester, John Whitehouse and Paul Daniels. Front row: Keith Hull, Robert Prior, Peter Massey and David Potts.

Fig.77.

I then started to go to the youth club at March End, this was run by Derek Buckley, a science teacher at March End.
In 1966 we went on holiday with the youth club to Exmouth camping. The cost was £10 for ten days with everything thrown in.
On leaving school I went to work at John Harpers, a cast iron foundry in Willenhall that's where I served an apprenticeship in pattern making. I spent 14 years of my working life there. By now a teenager, Monday nights were spent dancing at the Civic Hall and weekends at the Wood Hayes. That's where the first disco in Wednesfield was held

along with ultra violet lights; sadly now a fond memory and a heap of rubble. But of the music of the sixties, still my favourite era for music. I played football for John Harpers and Wednesfield Social. I had a reasonably successful career winning a number of trophies. My ultimate dream was to play at the Molineux but this was shattered, having got to the final of the JW Hunt Cup thinking that I was going to be playing at the Molineux, the Wolves grounds man decides to reseed the pitch, so it was back to Butlers on Springfield Road for the final in 1974 against Northicote OB.

Fig.78. John Harpers FC; Back row (L-R) Walter Wakeman (Chairman) Keith Longmore, Peter Higgins, Ken Lisseman, Keith Dunn, Ray Cooper, Alan Ray, Les Sephton, Bert Taylor (Manager). Front row: Alfie Tarbuck, Roger Bird, Brian Swift, Pete Massey, Tony Guest

In 1979 I was lucky enough to secure a position at Dowty, Boulton & Paul where I worked with some of the best craftsmen in the area. 32 years at the company doing various jobs, patternmaking, drilling, honing and class 1 De Burring. Working on numerous aircraft including EFA (Typhoon) JSF (Joint Strike Fighter) Mr CA (Tornado) Hawk A380 and my claim to fame was working on parts for Concorde.

In previous books various companies have been mentioned in the surrounding area, while little has been said about Boulton & Paul. Their aircraft the defiant is commemorated on the Battle of Britain Wall in Kent. The company has recently been taken over by the Moog aircraft group. I am still working there now after working there all those years you could say that I was happy there.
Well Pete I remember playing against you when I went to Neachells Lane School. I can remember that we hardly ever beat Woden Avenue at football. Yes we ended up meeting at March End School; can you remember some of those kids form your class?
Yes March End School did have the best looking girls in Wednesfield and some of them went to the youth club, run as you say by Derek Buckley. He was good with the science, remember those Bunsen burners?
That camping holiday £10 for 10 days, what a bargain. I never went because £10 was money then. Hey Pete we have all played at the Molineux in our dreams and some played for the Wolves in the band at half time. Thanks for your memories of Wednesfield Pete. I still reckon that I could get past you with a ball even today.

Anslows Shops

After Mr & Mrs Anslow died, their daughter Ruby ran it until her retirement. The butchers on the corner of Nordley Road and Frederick Road was Downings before Jervis's had it. On the opposite corner was a fruiterer – Tommy Jurdison. Mr and Mrs Jurdison senior ran it, they passed it on to their son Tom Junior and his wife.
At the top of Nordley Road turning right onto Vicarage Road was a sweet shop / newsagents owned by a Mr Harwood.
Up Vicarage Road about two thirds of the way up before the terraced houses; a sweet shop and general store that was owned by Mrs Tench.
The Army Camp was a REME Depot during the war and soldiers were there during the early fifties.

Fig.79. Council yard previously REME depot during the war.

Lily Daish-Cottage Homes

Many of the children who grew up at the Cottage Homes may remember Mr CJ and Mrs AM Daish who were well known and respected by the folk of Wednesfield for their long service at the Homes.

Mr Daish originated from the Isle of Wight while Mrs Daish came from Dorset, who worked as poor law officers (as it was known in those days).

In 1926 they came to Wednesfield with their daughter Marjorie and son Douglas (who later became my husband) to fill the post of assistant superintendent and assistant matron of the Homes.

Their living quarters were in the Lodge which was situated to the right of the gates as you entered, where new admissions and visitors had to book in and out. To the left of the gates was the Superintendent's office where he and Mr Daish administered the running of the Homes. The Lodge housed 14 – 16 older boys, their dormitories being on the upper floor.

Fig.80. The Lodge, Cottage Homes.

There were 20 acres allowing the homes to be mainly self-sufficient i.e. (Bakehouse) Tailors workshop, seamstress, shoe maker, cobbler and also a swimming pool, pigs were kept and there was also a horse called boxer who did the ploughing, there was also farming.

There was a school, later some did attend outside schools, only milk and eggs were brought in from a farm in Brewood on a daily basis. As reported in the Express & Star and Wolverhampton Chronicle Mr and Mrs Daish retired in 1949 after 23 years' service. They went to live in Penn where they remained until Mr Daish died in 1962; Mrs Daish died 10 years later when it was widely reported in the news that she died suddenly aged 84. Marjorie, their daughter passed away this year on 3rd June 2011.

Fig.81. Mr Daish attending plot at rear of homes.

Fig.82. Retirement from the Cottage Homes for Mr Daish.

Fig.83. Mr and Mrs Daish with daughter Marjorie.

Fig.84. Football team with shield 1933/34. Top row: Dick Taylor, Charlie Pursehouse, Sid Machin, Dave Butler, Ron Jervis, Bill Nield, Doug Hughes, Jack Tench. Second row: Jim Hadley, Bert Lewis, G Davies, Jim Smart, Dave Mason, Jack Edwards. Third row: Ken Smith, Bob Rogers, Doug Daish, Howard Jones, Stan Bissell, Phil Drury, Jack Morby. Bottom row: Les Cooper, Albert Morris, Harry Cook, Harry Morgan, Jim Moore.

Wednesfield Police Station

Wednesfield Police Station was a large house just over the Rookery Bridge on the right. The entrance had a window with a hatch to which all general public came for various reasons. The main door led to the 'charge room' which contained a switchboard, radio, sergeant and a civilian clerk, this room was where the officers coming on duty were paraded by the sergeant for their various assignments. The cells led immediately off to this room where any offenders were detained.
On the ground floor there were two other doors, one leading to the kitchen where the officers on duty cooked their breakfast etc… there was no canteen in those days. The other led to the inspector's private quarters where he lived with his wife and daughter. Upstairs housed the CID and typist, the rear of the premises had a separate building where the inspector worked along with his secretary. There was also kennels for stray dogs and a couple of vehicles and a motorcycle.

There were two sub-stations, one in Wood End and one in Essington where the officers visited Wednesfield Station daily with their reports. Wednesfield Police Station originally came under Staffordshire and was mainly responsible to Willenhall where the senior officers were deployed.
In around 1965-1966 in Stubby Lane a landlady was murdered by her lodger, who incidentally was deaf and dumb. I was on duty the day that he was brought into the charge room. The charge made was unclear as the interviews took place through an interpreter, where he was taken, what sentence he received was also unclear as it was all kept rather low key.
Around 1968 the station closed, one sergeant was left at the station for a short period to wind things up. Officers and staff were transferred to either Bilston or Dunstall Road, Wolverhampton. Wednesfields new Police Station in Alfred Squire Road was officially opened on the 8th October 1971 by Richard C Sharples Esq, the building contractors were JF Wooton of Bloxwich. The old Police Station was demolished in the early 1970s.
Thanks Lily for your memories of Wednesfield and the Cottage Homes and the good police force of old Wednesfield.

Evelyn Bailey

I first came to live in Wednesfield from South Wales in 1938. I went to Wood End School which was built at the same time as our house in Prestwood Avenue. It was like moving into a building site, but I enjoyed the school. Mr Fidler was headmaster and I was in Miss Williams's class. My brother was in the infants and the local bobby lived next door to the school. The Pheasant pub was run by Jack Wootons sister Elizabeth and the gardens went right back into our avenue, they were partly sold off after the war and built on.
We used to take walks over Campions fields as it had a right of way with stiles and was a short cut to Essington. Where the roundabout is now was Pinches shop and a Blacksmith and also an orchard opposite at the corner.
The Lancaster air crash, when that happened we were in the garden when it came over Bushbury direction. We ran over past the 'dump'

REME camp over the canal bridge to the Lichfield Road where it had crashed; everything was in bits and was being collected in bags (one small boy picked up something but threw it down again when he realised that it was a hand, he then ran off). There was another crash not far from there, it was a Spitfire but the pilot was unharmed (there was a TV programme about it a couple of years ago).

I went to Lichfield Road School at the age of 11 and a few pupils lived in Tithe Road so I suppose you do know them.

In your book you mention the Battle of Wodensfield (as it was taught us). Mr Forest our History and Geography teacher told us such a lot about it and said that if we went to the site (New Street Area) on the anniversary of the battle we would hear the sounds of the battle (I worked 30 years night duty at New Cross and never heard anything).

The pubs and churches mentioned reminded me of my Auntie Dora who visited us from Sheffield; she said that she had never been to anywhere that had so many pubs and Churches in such a small place.

Sam Reynolds who was a councillor and an ex-boxer kept The Angel or maybe The Tiger. The Regal was our Saturday morning delight, if we got there early and got the back row. We were nearly always put up in the circle when downstairs got full. The Smack we went to if we were hard up, the film always broke down and then the stamping of feet on the floor began. The poor manager rushed round threatening to throw everybody out.

Downings the butchers-my father had to provide chicken and rabbits to them during the war. This would give him the money so that he could feed us. Their Son Tony played in Bob White's band when we went dancing at the 'Stute'.

Doctor Bentley's wife was in charge of wool etc...and we had to go from the school to collect it so that we could knit for the forces, a lot of pupils used to go potato picking during the war instead of lessons.

One day we were in the playground at Lichfield Road School when a plane came over very low, we could see the pilot and we waved to him.

Mr Kingston our headmaster came out shouting to us to get in and go to the hall immediately. He was so upset and angry because the plane

was a German Reconisance plane and if he had a machine gun we could have all been dead.
The REME camp by the canal had a big gun we called Bertha and my father who was in the Home Guard worried when the German Planes were passing over towards Birmingham and Coventry in case they fired the gun as it was an ammunition dump and we would have all gone up in smoke. We did have one night when incendry bombs dropped in our street and three unexploded bombs were disarmed.
I remember having fish and chips from the wooden hut by the bus terminus and they were great. You say that you worked on the market for a while, well when it opened on the opposite side of the road to the Regal, we exchanged our van with Sam Reynolds' brother Harry for his car for a couple of months so he could transport his goods (another ex-boxer) but he gave it up after about 12 months. John Sleeuwenhook was part of the Harris family in Prestwood Avenue. I think his father was killed shortly after he was born and a uniform was made identical to his father, who was a captain (he looked great in it).
I wish that I had had a camera in those days; I would have had so many lovely photos. Sadly I didn't get one until I was working and married. And finally in the words of Bob Hope "Thanks for the memory".
Evelyn that was great. You can take the girl out of Wednesfield but you can't take Wednesfield out of the girl.

Charlotte Billingsley (Nee Newton)

I was born on the 15th February 1939 in the house next door to the Social Club in Bolton Road; then not long after I was born we moved to a house in Merrills Hall Lane to live with my Dad's dad.
There were only two houses down the lane; one was my Grandad's, the other belonged to the Taylor's but it was previously owned by a Miss Medcalf. My Granddad's house went with his job which was managing the sewer beds across the canal from where we lived.
I remember when the winters were bad, the kids from Hart Road used to come and we used to skate on the canal.
Right opposite our house was a big field which was called C and B Smiths with a wooden pavilion and from what I was told there was

football played on it. If you looked across the field you could see the firm of Jenks and Cattell's they used to make garden tools. I remember my mother telling me when the war was on the Lady's used to go with prams and wheelbarrows to pick coal off what was called the blue fly. After the war I went to Neachells Lane School until I was seven, then the council offered us a house in Moathouse Lane West. As my Grandad's house only had two bedrooms and my uncle had just come back from the Army, that's when I moved schools to Wood End. That's where I started to show an interest in Athletics. At the age of eleven I moved to Lichfield Road School where I started doing my running under the supervision of my PE teacher Mr Marlow. When I was in my last year at school that's when I started running for Wednesfield Athletics and for my school against other schools. We used to train on the field in Fibbersley in the week, then on Sunday mornings we used to train on the running track at Aldersley Stadium whilst it was just being built, that's when the club decided to join forces with Birchfield Harriers.

Fig.85. Charlotte at Merrills Hall Lane.

Fig.86. Lichfield Road School mid 50's.

Fig.87. A very determined looking Charlotte at Lillishal Hall.

Once a month we used to go to Lillishal Hall for weekend training where we met up with other Athletic clubs but when I was 18. I decided to give up my running because I was working full time at the Yale in Willenhall, there really was too much training every night.

Fig.88. Charlotte- training at Lilleshal Hall.

I got married in December 1959; our wedding was the first one to be allowed to have photos taken that was in St Thomas' Church. I have three children; two boys and a daughter. My daughter was born in 1963; I have photos of her in her pram taken on Wednesfield market with Councillor and MP Jennie Lee and the Mayoress of Wolverhampton.
Four and a half years later I had my first son John, two and a half years later my second son Malcolm was born; so this is just part of my life story spent in Wednesfield.
Oh Charlotte you could have made it. You could have been a great runner but like most folk there were more important things in life than running, maybe next time.

Rosalind Cooper nee Broomhall
I was born in 'The Village' in 1944 at the Post Office it was war time and rationing. I remember the back of the Post Office- the council yard. There was a sweet shop next door (Mrs Evans). My father (as most people did in those days) used to grow vegetables and used to get sweet jars from the sweet shop and buy blocks of salt for the winter (not healthy by today's standards).
It was a village then and everyone knew everyone. As I grew up my sister Gillian and I had saved hard to buy bikes which we eventually

bought from Woods in Rookery Street. They were our pride and joy, we went everywhere on our bikes Bridgnorth, The Wrekin and Kinver. My school days started at Woden Avenue then St Thomas' Church School, I remember the old Church school which is now where William Bentley Court now stands. We had various lessons in there but what I remember most was a slop bucket for left overs; enough to put you off for life. Whatever the weather we had PT and used King George's playing fields for 'Shinty' (which was like Hockey) also Tennis on the Courts and Netball on the playground at the new school. We had assembly in the Institute where I was always at the back being one of the tallest; the other two being Jennifer Porter and Barbara Hughes.

When I left school at 15 I went to work for my father until 1962 when I went to work at Tettenhall Wood Post Office; still riding my bike to and fro everyday even through Wolverhampton (wouldn't do it now). Wednesfield was a great place to be brought up in and holds many dear memories of many friends and acquaintances which I'll never forget.

Fig.89. Rosalind Cooper and friend. Carnival Day 1956. Vote for women.

Fig.90. Gillian Broomhall presenting a bouquet to a Wednesfield dignitary with Sammy Reynolds of 'The Angel' in the background.

Fig.91. Wednesflield Gala day 1962. Rosalind's father Stanley Broomhall shakes the paw of a dog.

Ian Fulford

I was born in Hickman Street, Wednesfield, in 1945. My parents (God rest them) were Bill and Sedda Fulford. North Street, New Street, Hickman Street, Cross Street and Charles Street, were bounded by Graiseley Lane, New Cross Hospital orchard, the cemetery, Wolverhampton Road and the canal. The area of terraced houses was built in the 19th century and initially housed families of trap makers, locksmiths, key smiths, and tinsmiths etc... who worked from small buildings in their back yards. Hickman Street ran where Torridge Drive is now. Charles Street ran along Thrushel Walk to Graiseley Lane; Cross Street was a continuation of Charles Street and then ran along Okement Drive; New Street ran from Graiseley Lane to Wolverhampton Road, across the top of Hickman Street; and North Street a continuation of Victoria Road down to Wolverhampton Road.

Fig.92. Hickman Street.

Fig.93.New Street around 1927. Star Public House on left, Blowers fish and chip shop lower down and also a drapers shop.

The more modern semi-detached houses which are still there, formed the corner of Cross Street and Hickman Street, and used to be home for Colin and Roy Foster; Billy and Barbara Harrison; Pauline, Ronnie and Alec Bartlell; Billy, Sandra, and Pamela Gibbons; plus the Taylors, Masons, Pursehouses and Kayes. Also in Cross Street lived Ray Smith and Marlene and Pearl Butler. In Charles Street lived Billy Rushton, Wendy Tomlinson, Bristows and Jacksons. In Hickman Street where there were more Jacksons and Tony and Margaret Evans, Peter Clare, and many more. More cousins, John, George and Jimmy Hinton lived in New Street. When the area was demolished in the late 1950's, these families departed to every other part of Wednesfield.

I remember playing 'Red Opple' down the length of the street, knocking on every dear to see how far you could run before someone opened their door. A typical shout was "I know who you are you little b******s! I'll tell your Dad when I see him!" Truth was it was too dark to see who it was. There was one lamp on the corner of Charles Street which seemed to have the power of a 40 watt bulb.

We used to play marbles (or marlies) on the patch of dirt on the corner of Cross Street, but when it started to get dark we would play 'jacks' under the street lamp until someone's mom would shout: "Come on now, school in the morning!" We'd make our short way home with a "See ya tomorra!" We played football in the street, the best pitch being in Cross Street (Chapel wall one side, garden walls opposite). We always seemed to play with a tennis ball. In the school holidays we would sometimes play football all day up the park. We would take bottles of water with us, or nip off home for a drink or sandwich, then rush to get back to the game which never stopped.
I also remember what seemed to be a 'three team tournament' between Billy Rushton, Ray Smith, Jeff Smith etc...) Horace Crutchley's team from Neachells Lane area (which included David Chester, Howard 'Ocker' Hollis etc...) and Johnny Rock's team from playing for Wednesfield Schools when I was 10, one of three representing Neachells Lane School (the other two were Freddy Cooper and Freddy Homer). The rest of the team were pupils of Wood End School including John Baker who was the best of us. We played against the schools of Darlaston, Wednesbury, Willenhall and Bilston.
I attended Neachells Lane School from 1950 – 1956, my teachers being (in order as far as I can remember) Miss Dovey, Miss Sidebottom, Miss Jameson, Mrs Prince (Infant Headmistress), Miss Bolas, Miss Bayliss, Mr Roberts and Mr Beddard. Headmaster was Mr Baxter.
In my class almost throughout were: Jack Hollinshead, Malcolm Crane, Terry Lovatt, Alan Smith, Alan Jones, Danny O' Donnell, Royston Fellows, Freddie Homer, Barbara Randel, Coral Benton, Christine Littlehales, Nora Williams to name a few. If you were there please forgive my memory lapse, we're all getting on a bit now.
Our family moved to the newly built Ashmore Park on Cup Final day 1956 (it was a panic to get the telly working) walking to and from school for the final year took a lot longer from Blackham Road than from Hickman Street. Moving to Ashmore Park began a whole new story; but being brought up with the 'salt of the earth' of Wednesfield set my standards for the future. Thank you to all of the aforementioned for being a part of my upbringing.

Well Ian you certainly remember the Hickman Estate pretty well because most people that I speak to cannot remember Charles Street. You must remember the fish and chip shop on the corner of Charles Street and Graiseley Lane fish and chips cooked in beef dripping. Fancy some now?

Fig.94. We believe this is Hickman Street Methodist Chapel. Cross Street is to the left, Charles Street to the right.

Ann Hunt- Photos of her time living in Wedenesfield.

Fig.95. Woden Avenue Junior School crowning of the School Queen 1948 (Diane Lee). On the left; Pat Morgan, on the right Ann Hunt.

Fig.96. Lichfield Road school play. Margaret George, Irene Percil, Rita Lathe, Mary Pickering, Ann Hunt, J Pearson, Olive, J Gilbert, B Spencer.

Fig.97. Wednesfield Carnival Queen 1950's (Patsy Tasker with her attendants Ann Hunt, Valerie Watts, Wendy Felton, Pat Huble (hidden).

Fig.98. Lichfield Road Infants School 1929, Beryl Picken fourth left bottom row. Eunice Close (teacher).

Fig.99. Trinity Methodist
Sunday School anniversary 1947. Brian Griffiths (tall lad at the back), Diane Griffiths (third right), Brian Whitehouse (holding his coat).

Fig.100. Trinity Methodist.
Alice Freeman, Cliff Johnson with his dog, Ken Freeman, Jill Wilson, Mrs Johnson (second from left), Ann Hunt (fifth left).

Fig.101. Wesleyan Church next to Pickering's prior to 1957. The Church was built in 1886 and opened on July 19th of the same year.

34. My bit of fun

Songs and what they really mean.

I love my dog (Cat Stevens) - Walk in the park.
I am a rock (Simon & Garfunkel) - Alcatraz.
Homeward Bound (Simon & Garfunkel) – Holidays.
The closest thing to crazy (Katie Melua) – Going to work.
Father and Son (Cat Stevens) – Facts of life.
Can't keep it in (Cat Stevens) – Guess.
Another Saturday night (Cat Stevens) - No money.
Peace Train (Cat Stevens) – Fell out with the missus.
Another brick in the wall (Pink Floyd) – Going to work / signing on.
Bridge over troubled waters (Simon & Garfunkel) - Gas bill.
Under Pressure (Queen and David Bowie) – Gas bill.
The Drugs don't work (The Verve) – Back ache.
Angels (Robbie Williams) – Meet up one day millions of years from now.
Just friends (Amy Winehouse) – Fancy bit down the street.
Old before I die (Robbie Williams) – Dead lucky.
Kids (Robbie Williams) – Who'd have em.
Sexed up (Robbie Williams) – Pretty woman.
Rainy days and Mondays always get me down (Carpenters) – Talk to Bob Geldof about Monday's he didn't like them either.
Don't look back in anger (Oasis) - ?
Yesterday once more (Carpenters) – Reading my books.
Calling occupants of interplanetary craft (Carpenters) – The recognised anthem of world contact day.

Quotes that mean something:

1. Those who know how to think need no teachers. (Ghandi).
2. We can all do more than what we think we can. (Eddie Izzard)
3. We come into this world with a pre-ordained destiny.

35. Armed Forces

I just thought readers should be able to take a look at these following photos; really speaking it's a last minute decision to put these in the book. Please take a look you might be able to recognise someone in the photos.

Fig.102.

Ypres Platoon. Regimental Depot the 22nd (Cheshire) Regiment 25th intake February to April 1955.

From L-R Back row – Ptes. Woodcock, Farrington, Whittaker, Livens, Hallworth, Bailey, Montgomery – Tomlinson, Steele, Ash, Ollier, Griffiths.

Third Row- Ptes. Leech, Peacock, King, Westray, Walker, Keegan, Lea, Carter, Duckett, Lovatt, Maybury, Tudor.

Second row- Ptes- Pickering, Kershaw, Whitehurst, Taylor, Hughes, Williamson, Thomson, Diable, Miller, Davenport, Lynch, Baker.

Front row – Ptes. Allman, Williams, Cpl Hadley, Cpl Pickford, Sgt Pinkard, Lt AFW Astle, Cpl Cottis, Thornton, Ptes Potts, Stanley, Beard.

Fig.103.

Ypres Platoon Regimental Depot the 22nd (Cheshire) Regiment 38th intake – 4th October to 12th December 1956.

From L-R Back row- Ptes, Jeffery, Farquhar, Sully, Peers, Smith, Harris, Holden, Jones (20) Brown, Morgan.

Centre row- Ptes Malone, Gill, Pavitt, Whittaker, Cook, Radcliffe, Duer, Wardle, Proctor, Storr.

Front row- Ptes Dale, Jones (37) Humphreys, Cpl Richardson, Sgt Lewis, Cpl Stanley, Ptes Vickers, Thelwall, Turner, Carlisle.

Fig.104.

Somme & Loos Squads 10th October 1957 intake depot; The South Staffordshire Regiment.

From L-R – Front Row- Secker M, McKechnie G, L/Cpl Timmins B, Stanley K, Cpl Ford A, Sgt Grimthe E, Lt M Hill, Sgt Lote D, Cpl Stanley WA, L/Cpl Hanslow E, Smithyman R, Willet B, Ward D, Fellows H.

Second Row- Handley B, Harrison C, Wortons C, Howells T, Birch G, Doleman L, Rowley F, Jackson L, Parker M, Horne B, Sears A, Butler T, Billingham F, Turner R, Swannick WA, Brammer PE, Harris JH.

Third Row- Miles K, Silvan D, Swain L, Robbins P, Massey A, Pate T, Knight R, Deelex T, Cordell B, Roper J, Jeavons T, Plant N, Sheridan P, Bailey D, Holyhead W.

Back row- Gallimore K, Lusted R, Jolly C, Flanagan D, Morris P, Westwood C, Philpot R, Hubball J, France W, Hughes M, Bowers D, Wood J, Gould B, Edge N.

Conclusion

Well I really hope that you have enjoyed this latest journey into Wednesfields past.

On doing research into this book I have once again met some very nice and friendly people from Wednesfield. In particular I would like to thank Elizabeth Smallshire for the use of some of her late husband John's photographs of Wednesfield. In 1978 John Smallshire wrote a book about Wednesfield.

I purchased this book way back then and I am still the proud owner of that book today, albeit a bit tattered but nonetheless I still refer to it when folk ask about the battle. John gave some really interesting facts about Wednesfields past, once again thank you Elizabeth and John Smallshire. It's been a great journey writing the books WEDNESFIELD OUR VILLAGE, THIS IS WEDNESFIELD OUR WEDNESFILED and now WEDNESFIELD OUR HERITAGE.

Thank you for joining me on 'our' journey through Wednesfield's past.

On a final note; I will compile all of the photographs of Wednesfield together to form a photo album; containing photos from all three books. To be published in 2012.

SD - #0035 - 070726 - C0 - 255/180/8 - PB - 9781780352213 - Gloss Lamination